BACKROADS & BYWAYS OF
NEW ENGLAND

Rocky Gorge, along the Kancamagus Highway in New Hampshire, is quiet and cool on a hot summer day.

BACKROADS & BYWAYS OF
NEW ENGLAND

Drives, Day Trips
& Weekend Excursions

Karen T. Hammond

The Countryman Press
Woodstock, Vermont

We welcome your comments and suggestions.

Please contact

Editor
The Countryman Press
P.O. Box 748
Woodstock, VT 05091

or e-mail countrymanpress@wwnorton.com.

Backroads & Byways of New England
ISBN 978-0-88150-901-4

Book design by Hespenheide Design
Map by Erin Greb Cartography, © The Countryman Press
Interior and cover photos by Nathaniel Hammond
Composition by Chelsea Cloeter

Published by The Countryman Press, P.O. Box 748, Woodstock, VT 05091

Distributed by W. W. Norton & Company, Inc., 500 Fifth Avenue, New York, NY 10110

Printed in the United States of America

10 9 8 7 6 5 4 3 2 1

*For my mother, wise enough to know that both
the journey and the destination matter,
and for Alice, Molly, and Lucy,
the latest generation of New Englanders.*

If you don't know where you are going,
any road will get you there.
—*Lewis Carroll*

When you come to a fork in the road, take it.
—*Yogi Berra*

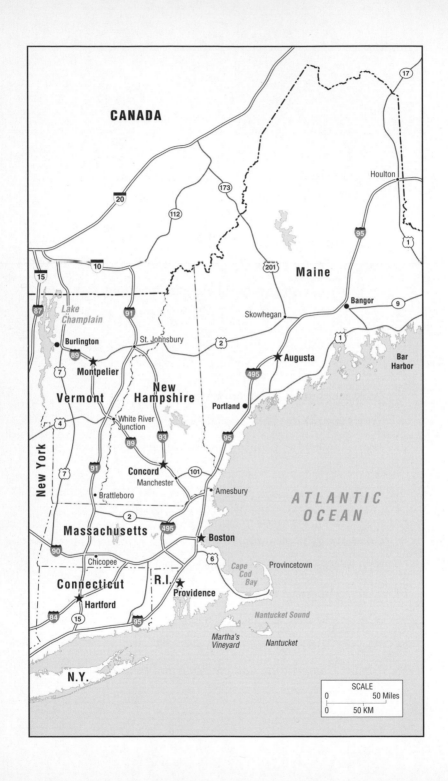

Contents

Acknowledgments 9

Introduction 11

1. Connecticut: *A Maritime Journey* 17

2. Connecticut: *The Quiet Corner* 31

3. Rhode Island: *East Bay and the Sakonnet Peninsula* 45

4. Massachusetts: *The North Shore* 57

5. Massachusetts: *The Mohawk Trail* 77

6. New Hampshire: *The Lakes Region* 91

7. New Hampshire: *Cruising the Kancamagus Highway* 105

8. New Hampshire: *Antique Alley* 115

9. Vermont: *Quechee and Beyond* 125

10. Vermont: *Bennington to Brattleboro on the Molly Stark Byway* 141

11. Maine: *The Schoodic Peninsula and Down East* 155

12. Maine: *Aroostook County* 173

13. Maine: *The Rangeley Lakes Region* 189

14. Maine: *The Sebago Lake Region* 203

15. Maine: *Damariscotta and the Pemaquid Peninsula* 219

Acknowledgments

Sincere thanks to everyone at Countryman Press, especially editorial director Kermit Hummel, managing editor Lisa Sacks, copy editor Melissa Dobson, and acquisitions editor Kim Grant. I appreciate the input of several freelancing colleagues, including Jackie Dishner and Lisa Halvorsen, and the technical assistance of Barry Gauger. Susana Soltero Liebow, Nancy Marshall, Lori Moretti, Melissa Rubin, Rebecca Schinas, Charlene Williams, and the representatives of the convention and visitor bureaus in all six New England states provided helpful background information. Many thanks!

On the road trip of life, it helps to have a traveling companion, especially one with a sense of direction and a sense of humor. Special thanks to my husband, photographer Nathaniel Hammond, for navigating us through the winding roads and hidden corners of the New England that both our families have loved for generations, and for dealing with snow, floods, blazing heat, and one crotchety moose while taking all the photos for this book.

Introduction

There is a little bit of New England in all Americans—those whose families have been here for generations and those who have recently arrived on our shores. Much of America's history began here, after all, with the arrival of a hardy group of Separatists seeking a better life. Each fall we celebrate their fortitude with a holiday focused not on gift giving or a particular religious or political belief, but on giving thanks and gathering together with our families.

Drive through New England in the autumn of the year and here are some of the things you will find: farm stands heaped with a late harvest of apples, potatoes, pumpkins, and squash; maple trees blazing crimson and gold in the slanted light; dried cornstalks tied together to bracket the sturdy wooden doors of centuries-old homes; country fairs, festivals, and baked-bean suppers.

Autumn slides swiftly into winter in this part of the country, and one morning you awake to lacy tracings of ice on the windows. A few days later, the first snow falls. New Englanders spend a lot of time talking about the weather, especially in the northernmost parts of the region. Old-timers, just slightly tongue-in-cheek, tell visitors, "We have two seasons: winter and the Fourth of July."

But weather rarely slows things down. Plows and sand trucks wait at the ready in every New England city, village, and town, and most of the time it's business and school as usual, even after a heavy snowstorm.

Winter sports like skiing, snowboarding, tobogganing, and ice skating bring many travelers back year after year. Few things compare to returning to a country inn after a day on the slopes and being greeted by a roaring fire in a great stone fireplace or a bowl of stew in a convivial pub.

Or, drive here to enjoy the winter holidays. Stores pull out all the stops to decorate, and virtually every home sports a wreath—usually balsam or another fir, simply decorated with a big red bow. But as you drive along, watch for creative homeowners' twists on the traditional, such as seashell wreaths in Maine and the cranberry wreaths so popular in Massachusetts.

Along wintry back roads you may come across people gathering bouquets of scarlet winterberries or cutting down one of the "Charlie Brown" Christmas trees so beloved by New Englanders—slightly crooked, often harboring a vacated bird's nest (said to bring good luck), and fragrant with the smell of a winter forest. A day later, catch a glimpse of one of these trees in a lighted window and you'll find it decorated with Grandma's antique glass ornaments, crocheted snowflakes, and children's construction-paper angels.

Winter gives way to mud season—sometimes called "the fifth season"—which in turn gives way to a glorious spring. Owners of antiques shops dust off treasures accumulated over the winter, seasonal restaurants and lobster and clam shacks open, and botanical gardens welcome early visitors. Although it's impossible to give a lot of space to cosmopolitan Boston in a book about backroads and byways—it is, after all, the hub of New England (in days gone by, Bostonians claimed it was the hub of the universe)—some readers will no doubt add Boston to their itineraries or begin their tours of New England in the city, and thus should note that two important spring rites take place here: the first home game at Fenway Park, America's oldest professional baseball field, and the return of the Swan Boats, owned and operated by the same family for more than 130 years, to the Boston Public Garden. With the weather moderate, and before the summer influx of visitors, spring may be the best time to take a break from driving and stroll through America's Walking City.

It's also a great time of year for foodies to come to New England. Chefs lighten their menus using seasonal, local produce, and as spring progresses, it's warm enough to picnic in a park or on the cliffs beside a lighthouse, or to hike New Hampshire's White Mountains or the Green Mountains of Vermont with a backpacked lunch to eat along the way. Hard-shelled lobsters, which many aficionados prefer, are available in coastal towns throughout New England; as spring wears on and the lobsters shed, much of the catch will be soft-shelled (but still delicious), and the price for hard shells will rise accordingly.

And finally it's summer—all too fleeting in New England but wonderful while it lasts. This is the time for boating, swimming (by June in Connecticut, by August—maybe—in Maine); fishing; leisurely drives through the mountains and along the coast; craft fairs on village greens; quiet evenings chatting with other guests on the deck of a bed & breakfast or historic inn; and memorable Fourth of July celebrations complete with rootin'-tootin' parades, fairs, and fireworks.

Chances are that travelers with special interests will find something to intrigue them along New England's byways. Museums range from the vast Mystic Seaport Museum in Mystic, Connecticut, to the elegant Peabody-Essex Museum in Salem, Massachusetts. There are even tiny museums in many lighthouses, which devotees will find in every New England state including Vermont, despite its lack of an ocean shoreline.

Artists have long been attracted to New England's mountains, lakes, and rocky shores, and virtually every hamlet has an art gallery or two, while music lovers will find everything from symphony orchestras to local musicians playing on Friday nights on a town bandstand while children march around with lightsticks.

And what of New Englanders themselves? Are they the dour, insular, provincial people they're sometimes portrayed to be? The kind who, when you're lost on a back road, will insist that you "can't get theah from heah?" It's true that native New Englanders tend to be quiet, self-contained, and respectful of their own privacy and that of others. This last trait may perpetuate the myth that they are standoffish. Particularly in rural New England, residents may wait for you to say good morning, ask for directions, or otherwise make the first move; after all, they don't want to intrude on your personal space. Strike up a conversation, however, and chances are that you will make a garrulous acquaintance; make a friend of a New Englander and he or she will likely be a friend for life.

Dining can be one of the most memorable experiences of a New England trip. From "stuffies" (stuffed clams) in Rhode Island to scrod and baked beans in Massachusetts to Maine's famous lobsters—boiled, broiled, stuffed, heaped into lobster rolls, or incorporated into bisques and casseroles—regional cuisine will be a highlight of your stay. Ice cream lovers will be interested to know that New Englanders make some of the best ice cream in the country and consume it in vast quantities despite the long, cold winters, with coffee ice cream the hands-down favorite in Rhode Island. And no trip to this region would be complete without taking in a church or community supper. Watch bulletin boards and local newspapers for chowder suppers and baked-bean suppers, and many that offer comfort cooking such as ham, hot dogs, casseroles, coleslaw, and fabulous homemade pies using native apples, cranberries, or blueberries.

Diners, family-style restaurants, seafood shacks, and restaurants focusing on traditional New England fare abound, but those seeking a fabulous gourmet meal will not be disappointed. Some of the most respected chefs and restaurants in the country can be found not just in Boston, Providence, and Portland—all notable culinary cities in New England—but also in small towns and villages throughout the six-state area. Menus often boast locally raised meats, seafood caught just hours earlier, local produce, and herbs grown in gardens just outside the kitchen door.

Readers will note that pricing categories have been used in the accommodation and dining listings at the end of each chapter. These should be considered general guidelines and are subject to change. Accommodations are listed as inexpensive (to $150 per night, double), moderate ($150–250), and expensive ($250 or more). Keep in mind that prices tend to be higher near popular tourist areas, and all prices may rise during peak travel seasons and holidays. On the other hand, in rural areas it's often easy to find clean and comfortable accommodations for well under $100 at any time of year.

Dining prices are listed as inexpensive (dinner entrées available under $15), moderate ($15–$25), and expensive ($25 and up). Again, prices may fluctuate with the season.

Always call the hotel or restaurant or check the website to confirm current prices and inquire about specials and packages, which may offer substantial savings. Reservations are a good idea at any time of year.

Other practical considerations: When traveling in remote areas, be sure to bring current maps (I recommend DeLorme maps) as well as a GPS. You'll find both helpful in rural sections of New England. Always bring water and a few snacks, since restaurants can be few and far between, and don't forget the insect repellent, sunblock, and a small first-aid kit. Remember that New England is famous for changeable weather, so even in summer keep rain gear, long pants, and a sweater where you can reach them easily. Rubber-soled shoes are a must for walking along New England's bumpy sidewalks and cobblestone streets. And if you plan to hike, check with an outfitter to be sure you have the necessary gear; know your physical limits; and always inform a contact about when and where you are hiking and when you plan to return.

Whatever your personal interests, whatever season you travel here, chances are the backroads and byways of New England will take you someplace memorable.

Karen Hammond

The Old Lighthouse Museum in Stonington Borough. Each year a special exhibit focuses on one aspect of Stonington's history.

Connecticut:
A Maritime Journey

Estimated length: Hartford to Stonington, about 65 miles, plus area tour of about 35 miles.

Estimated time: Hartford to Stonington, about 90 minutes. Allow a half day to two days to tour the area.

Getting there: From Hartford, take Route 2 East to Route 11 South. Turn left onto Route 82, then right onto Route 85. Take Route 85 to I-95 North; follow I-95 North to Exit 91, Stonington. Follow signs into town.

Highlights: Although much of present-day Connecticut is highly urbanized, the Stonington-Mystic area retains its traditional New England ambiance and its bond with its seafaring past. It is here that brave townspeople, greatly outnumbered by an invading British fleet, successfully defended **Stonington** during the War of 1812. And it is here, along the Mystic shoreline, that vast shipyards once built oceangoing ships, local men and boys signed on as sailors—some never to return—and whalers set out in search of right whales whose oil helped keep the lights of New England, and the world, burning. Those who made their fortunes in these industries built the sturdy homes that blend with the area's natural beauty. Anyone who loves the sea will enjoy **Mystic Seaport** and the **Mystic Aquarium & Institute for Exploration.** Boat enthusiasts, history buffs, and those who enjoy the out-of-doors will all find plenty to explore. Expect to find parts of this area bustling in summer but quieter the rest of the year.

In the mid-1800s great clipper ships—fast, three-masted, square-rigged cargo ships—sailed from the Mystic area carrying goods all over the world. The region's written history, however, begins two centuries earlier, when the first European settlers arrived, in 1654, settling on land that had been inhabited by members of the Native American Pequot tribe for generations. Just as the word *Connecticut* is derived from the Native American *Quinnehtukqut,* meaning "beside the tidal river," the name *Mystic* comes from the Native American *Missi-tuk,* meaning, approximately, "a great tidal river with waves whipped by the winds." The area remains very much tied to its maritime history, and its most popular attractions honor that long heritage.

A good place to begin a journey in this area is in the attractive **Borough of Stonington,** whose first settlers arrived from the Plymouth Colony in the mid-1600s. One early arrival established a trading post and other homesteaders soon followed. Although Stonington was originally a farming community, over time its citizens became more and more oriented toward the sea, and it became a village of whalers, sealers, and shipbuilders. Today the harbor is home to the last remaining commercial fishing fleet in Connecticut.

Stonington is proud of the defense it launched during the War of 1812, when citizens stood up to an attack by British ships determined to take over the town. Brave townspeople refused to budge, and held off some 160 British guns with nothing more than three cannons and plenty of Yankee grit. Three days later, battered and demoralized, the British fleet sailed away. Some historians consider the Americans' standoff one of the turning points of the war.

Head down narrow Water Street and check out the shops, boutiques, and cafés before the street dead-ends at the Stonington Point parking lot and little duBois Beach. From the parking lot, where photographers angle for the perfect shot no matter what the weather, there is a clear view of Fishers Island in New York and Watch Hill in Rhode Island. In the distance, the ferry to Block Island, Rhode Island, passes by.

Turning back onto Water Street, you'll see the **Old Lighthouse Museum** on the right. With on-street parking at a premium, it's wise to leave the car in the parking lot at the point and walk the few steps back to the lighthouse. Active from 1840 to 1889, the lighthouse is built of materials from an earlier lighthouse nearby. The existing lighthouse, in turn, was deactivated after being replaced by a beacon on the harbor breakwater, and since 1927 has been home to the museum of the Stonington Historical Society. Several rooms are filled with memorabilia from Stonington's past and provide an interesting look at the lives of local shipbuilders, merchants, and tradespeople. The museum also houses a fourth-order Fresnel lighthouse lens. The lighthouse tower is open to the public, and those who climb to the top on a clear day are rewarded with spectacular views. A little museum shop sells nautical items.

A good place to stop for lunch or dinner is **Noah's,** in the center of town, a local hot spot even on the coldest winter day. In the evening, the two small rooms are packed; a handsome wooden bar accommodates those waiting for a table. A couple of musicians entertain on occasion, and all in all it's a great place to chat with locals while enjoying excellent food and generous drinks.

Take time to drive through Stonington's narrow streets past lovely 18th- and 19th- century Greek Revival and Federal-style homes, mostly built with money made from shipping and seal hunting, both once lucrative industries here. Many of these old homes are set just a few feet from the street, a result of roads being widened again and again over the centuries to meet the demands of contemporary traffic. On North Water Street (Route 1-A) you'll find the **Captain Nathaniel B. Palmer House**, a National Historic Landmark and outstanding example of Victorian architecture overlooking Stonington Harbor. Built by the famous "Captain Nat," discoverer of a previously uncharted area of the Antarctic, and his seafaring brother, Alexander Palmer, the home is especially noted for its beautiful woodwork.

If you'd like to stay overnight in Stonington, you'll find a quiet retreat at the **Inn at Stonington**, a bed & breakfast with views of the waterfront. The inn has bicycles to loan for easy access to duBois Beach.

To continue your journey, take Route 1 South into downtown Mystic. In warm weather, you'll find Mystic buzzing with tourists and traffic, but it's a vital stop because of all there is to see and do. The **Inn at Mystic**, located at the junction of Routes 1 and 27, is an ideal place from which to explore the entire Stonington-Mystic area. It's just far enough from the stores and restaurants to be quiet and peaceful, yet close enough so that you can leave the car here and walk into town.

With its 15-acre grounds and intriguing history, the inn is practically a destination in itself. The inn began as a motel, which still exists, but over time the owners purchased nearby buildings, and today there are several kinds of guest rooms on the property. Among these are rooms in a mansion built in 1904 by Katherine Haley, widow of an owner of New York's Fulton Fish Market, and now listed on the National Register of Historic Places. The nearby Gatehouse was erected by a later owner of the Haley mansion, financier and bon vivant Frederick Mosel, who was a friend of the actor Humphrey Bogart. In July 1945 Bogart and Lauren Bacall honeymooned in the Gatehouse. Although the building has undergone renovations, a portion of the honeymooners' accommodations is still used as a guest bedroom whose ambiance will give any film-lover a thrill. Book this room and you'll be overcome with a desire to curl your hair into a pageboy and whistle, or don a fedora and growl, "Here's looking at you, kid."

Yet another building houses the inn's **Flood Tide Restaurant,** recipient of many culinary awards. Guests and the public can enjoy a very civilized afternoon tea here every day at 4 PM. In summer, English gardens bloom throughout the property, which has glorious views of Mystic Harbor and Long Island Sound. It takes little imagination to look out over the water and envision the sloops, clipper ships, and whalers of yesteryear sailing past. Innkeeper Jody Dyer, a member of a well-known family of New England innkeepers who also own the renowned Harraseeket Inn in Freeport, Maine, shows guests around the property accompanied by canine concierges named Bogie and Blue.

Shortly after the Inn at Mystic as you drive or walk into town, you'll pass the **Mystic Depot Welcome Center** on the left. Stop here for a map, brochures, and public restrooms.

Exactly where Mystic begins and ends seems to be a conundrum to just about everyone, including the local who explained, "Well, it's pretty confusing, but people who live in Mystic know where they are and that's what counts." Technically Mystic is an area (with its own zip code) that lies partly in Stonington on the east side of the Mystic River and partly in Groton on the west side. An old **bascule bridge** (drawbridge) spans the river, surrounded on both sides by shops and restaurants.

A loud blast announces each bridge opening and closing. In the busy summer months, allow time to sit in traffic while the bridge opens, boats glide through, and the entire process is repeated in reverse to bring the span back down again. Because the 1922 bridge's mechanical workings are visible, the opening and closing are actually quite entertaining. Children seem

The Mystic Depot Welcome Center, also an Amtrak train station, once served as a model for a train depot built by American Flyer.

especially taken by the whole process involving wheels, counterweights, and other moving parts, and of course an ice cream cone from the **Mystic Drawbridge Ice Cream Café** adds to the fun. While meandering through the downtown area, take time to stop in at some of the little shops; **Peppergrass & Tulip**, a few steps beyond the café, offers funky jewelry and other accessories as well as dresses and decorative items with Victorian flare.

Many travelers come to Mystic specifically to get a glimpse of **Mystic Pizza,** just up the street from the bridge on the west side. Hollywood made the pizza shop famous and even borrowed its name for the iconic movie that starred a young Julia Roberts, although interior scenes were actually shot on a set when the real building proved to be too small. No matter; the pizza is still "A Slice of Heaven" as Roberts's T-shirt proclaimed in the movie. Waitstaff wear similar T-shirts today. Lines for a slice can be long in the summer months, but the pizza is worth the wait.

An interesting side trip from Mystic, **Noank** is a seaside village that evokes the rural Connecticut of days gone by, although it, too, can be busy

Mystic Pizza still draws sightseers more than two decades after the movie of the same name was filmed in Mystic.

in the peak summer months. To reach Noank, head west across the bascule bridge and turn left onto Route 215. After about 2.4 miles, turn left onto Mosher Avenue and into town. Narrow streets wind past the harbor, where both fishing and pleasure boats bob in the water. In season, stop at **Abbott's Lobster in the Rough** for a hot lobster roll or Abbott's version of a New England clambake, which starts with chowder and ends with lobster and all the fixings. Seating is outside at picnic tables, some of them under tents. You can bring your own beer or wine. The nearby **Costello's Clam Shack** serves up all things fried, especially local seafood.

Thus fortified, it's time to explore some of the excellent museums in this area. Returning to Route 215, turn left and after about 2 miles, turn left onto Route 1 toward Groton. En route you'll pass by small residential areas and, later, the inevitable strip malls and fast-food restaurants. Continue straight when you pass under I-95, at which point you will be on Route 12

DINING WITH ABBOTT AND COSTELLO

It would make a great story, but the late comedy team of Abbott and Costello of "Who's on First?" fame didn't retire to the small town of Noank, Connecticut, to open up a lobster restaurant and a clam shack. (The mind boggles to think about Lou Costello and a live lobster anywhere near each other.) Abbott's was founded in the 1940s by a man named Ernie Abbott and later bought by a loyal customer, Jerry Mears, who kept the restaurant's name. When another Noank restaurant folded, Mears decided to take over the nearby site. An employee jokingly told Mears that since he already owned Abbott's, he should open a new restaurant called Costello's. Recognizing a clever idea, Mears did just that and now Abbott's and Costello's are among the most popular casual eateries in the area.

North. Follow signs to the Submarine Force Museum to visit the historic *Nautilus,* the world's first nuclear-powered submarine. Launched January 21, 1954, in 1958 *Nautilus* became the first ship to cross the North Pole. *Nautilus* was decommissioned in 1980 after traveling half a million miles. The self-guided tour of the submarine and adjoining museum provide an interesting look at US naval history.

Return to Mystic via Route 12 to Route 1 where, if you have a special interest in the sea, you'll want to allow a full day at **Mystic Seaport.** A re-creation of a 19th-century seafaring community, Mystic Seaport's 17 acres of permanent and special exhibits cover virtually every aspect of 19th-century life along the Connecticut seacoast. You might join a sing-along of sea chanties, for example, listen in on a discussion of shipwrecks by a maritime author, or try your hand at scrimshaw carving or knot tying ("If you can't tie a knot, tie a lot," as the coastal saying goes). A ride on the museum's steamboat *Sabino* is a fun way to see a bit of Connecticut from the water.

Permanent exhibits include "Voyages: Stories of America & the Sea," with hundreds of original maritime artifacts; displays devoted to yachting and competitive rowing; a marvelous collection of figureheads and ships' carvings; a whaleboat exhibit filled with gear used by American whalers in the 1880s; the restored captain's stateroom and officers' mess from the 244-ft. sailing ship *Benjamin F. Packard,* which spent 20 years hauling goods around Cape Horn; and the North Boat Shed, with 500 small boats built between 1850 and 1950. Other permanent exhibits include the "*Thames* Keel and Shipbuilding Exhibit," displaying the 92-ft. keel assembly from the

Visitors can take a free, self-guided tour of the Nautilus *submarine housed at the Submarine Force Museum in Groton.*

whaling ship *Thames*; the Maritime Art Gallery, with displays of contemporary marine art; a scale model of Mystic River in 1870, complete with buildings and shipyards and teeny ships tied up along the docks; and the Treworgy Planetarium, where you can identify stars and planets, use a sextant, and learn how sailors plotted their journeys by celestial navigation long before radar and GPS.

The whaling ship *Charles W. Morgan,* now the last remaining American wooden whaling ship, was built in 1841 in New Bedford, Massachusetts, and sailed until 1921. Now berthed at Mystic Seaport, the ship offers a glimpse of what life was like for sailors at the height of the whaling era. You can view the crew's and captain's quarters, the ovens and kettles where whale blubber was rendered into oil, and the barrels where the oil was stored prior to being shipped to faraway places to light the lamps of the world.

There's still more to learn about the sea at the **Mystic Aquarium & Institute for Exploration.** Here you'll get up close and personal with creatures that live beneath or beside the water, such as beluga whales and all kinds of penguins, learn to differentiate between a seal and a sea lion, observe fish, turtles, and other sea creatures, and enjoy marine theater shows and hands-on exhibits. For traveling families, the aquarium provides hours of enjoyment. A café and a picnic area are on the premises.

The aquarium's Institute for Exploration, founded by Dr. Robert Ballard, discoverer of the remains of RMS *Titanic,* specializes in deep-sea archaeology using the latest robotic advances and remote-controlled vehicles. Don't miss the "Challenges of the Deep" exhibit, which highlights Ballard's recent discoveries. Viewing items such as an intact amphora hoisted to land after centuries underwater is a memorable experience.

All the museums have excellent stores if you're looking for a memento of your visit, but while you're here at the seaport or aquarium, you may also want to check out the nearby **Olde Mystick Village**. In this shopping area built to replicate a Colonial village, you'll find everything from sunglasses to Irish jewelry to Early American primitives or gardening supplies as well as plenty of places to stop and rest or get a bite to eat. Depending on the time of year, you may hear a band concert or a barbershop quartet, or watch a juggler perform. Special events take place during the summer months and winter holidays.

A highlight of any tour of this area—and a chance to commune with nature after long hours in the car—is a hike through the **Pequotsepos Nature Center**, a 300-acre sanctuary with 8 miles of walking trails that meander through woods and meadows. To get there from the aquarium or Old Mystick Village, go east on Coogan Boulevard to Jerry Browne Road, then right on Pequotsepos Road. Open year-round, springtime, when the wildflower and butterfly gardens bloom, is an especially pretty time here. If

---

THE STORY OF SCRIMSHAW

Mystic Seaport's "Voyages: Stories of America & the Sea" exhibit includes more than 100 pieces of scrimshaw, all excellent examples of this art form by New England sailors who created decorative items from the teeth, bones, and baleen of whales. Herman Melville discusses scrimshaw in his famous whaling tale, *Moby-Dick.* Intricately etched whales' teeth are perhaps the best-known examples of scrimshaw, but sailors also made toys, pie crimpers and other kitchen tools, and even personal items such as corset stays. Scrimshaw is a reminder of long, lonely nights on the vast ocean, when sailors turned their thoughts to faraway homes and their hands to making souvenirs for the wives and sweethearts they hoped to see again one day.

---

you have nature lovers on your gift list, a charming store on the premises carries field guides of all kinds, gardening books, nature puzzles, and a host of other objects for those who enjoy the out-of-doors. It's a pleasant place to stretch your legs before ending your tour of this corner of Connecticut. Return to I-95 South to begin your journey back to Hartford.

IN THE AREA

Accommodations

Hampton Inn and Suites, 6 Hendel Drive, Mystic. Phone: 860-536-2536; www.hamptoninn.hilton.com. Moderate.

Inn at Mystic, Junction of Routes 1 & 27, Mystic. Phone: 800-237-2415; www.innatmystic.com. Moderate.

Inn at Stonington, 60 Water Street, Stonington. Phone: 860-535-2000; www.innatstonington.com. Moderate.

Dining

Abbott's, 117 Pearl Street, Noank. Phone: 860-536-7719; www.abbotts-lobster.com. Open for lunch and dinner, May–Oct. Inexpensive to moderate.

Costello's, 145 Pearl Street, Noank. Phone: 860-572-2779; www.costellos clamshack.com. Open for lunch and dinner, May–Oct. Inexpensive.

Flood Tide Restaurant at Inn at Mystic, Junction of Routes 1 & 27, Mystic. Phone: 860-536-8140; www.innatmystic.com. Uses as much organic and natural food as possible. Beautiful views of the Mystic River. Open for afternoon tea and dinner. Moderate to expensive.

Mystic Drawbridge Ice Cream Café, 2 West Main Street, Mystic. Phone: 860-572-7978; www.mysticdrawbridgeicecream.com. Many flavors of ice cream plus sandwiches, salads, and paninis. Open daily 9–11 in summer; 9–10 in winter. Inexpensive.

Mystic Pizza, 56 West Main Street, Mystic. Phone: 860-536-3700; www.mysticpizza.com. Open daily for lunch and dinner. Inexpensive.

Noah's, 113 Water Street, Stonington. Phone: 860-535-3925; www.noahs
finefood.com. Open daily except Mon. for breakfast, lunch, and dinner.
Inexpensive to moderate.

Attractions and Recreation

Captain Nathaniel B. Palmer House, 40 Palmer Street at the corner of
Route 1-A, Stonington. Phone: 860-535-8445; www.stoningtonhistory
.org/palmer.htm. This elegant home with its 16 rooms and 10-ft.-wide
front doors showcases the financial success of its owners. An eight-sided
cupola reached by a winding staircase was probably a popular place from
which to watch ships sailing into port or departing on long journeys. Take
a peek at the summer kitchen, where meals were cooked during the
hottest months, and the sweet child's room, complete with toys typical of
the mid-1800s. Open May–Oct., Wed.–Sun., 1–5. Combination ticket
with Lighthouse Museum: Adults, $8; children $5.

Denison Pequotsepos Nature Center, 109 Pequotsepos Road., Mystic.
Phone: 860-536-1216; www.dpnc.org. Open daily 9–5 except Sun. 10–4.
Adults, $8; ages 12 and under and 65 and over, $5.

Mystic Aquarium & Institute for Exploration, 55 Coogan Boulevard,
Mystic. Phone: 860-572-5955; www.mysticaquarium.org. You'll come
away knowing more about the sea and its denizens than you could ever
have imagined. Open daily except major holidays. Dec.1–Feb. 28, 10–5;
Mar. 1–Oct. 31, 9–6; Nov. 1–30, 9–5. Adults, $26; seniors, $23; children
3–17, $19; under 2, free. All tickets are good for three consecutive days,
with validation.

Mystic Seaport, 75 Greenmanville Avenue, Mystic. Phone: 1-888-973-
2767; www.mysticseaport.org. Open late Mar. through Columbus Day,
daily 9–5. Winter hours: Thurs.–Sun. 10–4. Closed some holidays. Day-
time rides on the coal-fired steamboat *Sabino,* offered mid-May to mid-
Oct., leave on the half hour from 11:30–4:30. Built as a passenger ferry in
1908 in Maine, *Sabino* sailed along Maine's Damariscotta River before
being moved to Mystic Seaport. It is one of a handful of remaining wood-
en coal-fired steamboats still in operation. For a ride aboard *Sabino,* Mystic Seaport admission is required, plus adults, $5.50; ages 6–17, $4.50; 5
and under, free. Ninety-minute evening cruises beginning at 5:30 do not

Mystic Aquarium and Institute for Exploration

require Seaport admission. (Additional times added on Sat. from late June through early Sept.; call for details.) Weeknights: Adults, $12; Ages 6–17, $10. Add $2 for weekend tickets. Children 5 and under always free.

Old Lighthouse Museum, 7 Water Street, Stonington. Phone: 860-535-1440; www.stoningtonhistory.org/light.htm. Try to visit on a clear day, when the views from the lighthouse tower are quite spectacular. Open May–Oct., 10–5. Combination ticket with Captain Nathaniel B. Palmer House: Adults, $8; children, $5.

Submarine Force Museum and *Nautilus* Submarine, One Crystal Lake Road, Groton. Phone: 1-800-343-0079; www.ussnautilus.org. Those traveling with children should check the website for special events that will interest pint-sized sailors. Open May 1–Oct. 1, 9–5; Nov. 1–Apr. 30, 9–4. Closed every Tues., major holidays, and one or two weeks in spring and fall; may also close in inclement weather. Call for details. Free admission.

Shopping

Olde Mystick Village, Route 27 and Coogan Boulevard, Mystic. Phone: 860-536-4941; www.oldmysticvillage.com. Open year-round, daily 10–6, except Sun. 11–5.

Pepper Grass & Tulip, 30 West Main Street, Mystic. Phone: 860-536-1516.

Other Contacts

Mystic Depot Welcome Center, 2 Roosevelt Avenue, Mystic. Phone: 860-572-1102; www.mysticchamber.org.

Stonington information: www.stoningtonboroughct.com.

Stonington historical information: www.stoningtonhistory.org.

A statue in Putnam, a small town filled with antiques shops

CHAPTER

2

Connecticut: The Quiet Corner

Estimated length: About 45 miles from Hartford to North Woodstock; about 60 miles to tour the Quiet Corner.

Estimated time: One hour from Hartford to North Woodstock. Allow at least a morning or afternoon to explore the area.

Getting there: From Hartford take Route 44 East and turn north on Route 198 through Kenyonville. Turn right on Route 197 to North Woodstock, then south on Route 169 to Woodstock.

Highlights: Come to this peaceful corner of northeast Connecticut when you want to get away from the hustle and bustle of life. You'll enjoy a peaceful drive through a bit of bucolic New England that was once common and is now all too rapidly disappearing. Route 169, a designated National Scenic Byway, winds through a Connecticut so serene that if you've just arrived here from busy Hartford, you may find it difficult to believe you're still in the same state. Portions of the Quiet Corner lie within an area known as the Last Green Valley, a swath of mostly undeveloped land stretching between Washington, DC, and Boston that is noted for its pastoral scenery and focus on agriculture. That agricultural heritage is celebrated every year at the **Woodstock Fair.** For all its quietude and small size, northeastern Connecticut is rich in historic sites such as the **Prudence**

Crandall Museum and the **Nathan Hale Homestead,** and great natural beauty. To see it at its best, visit from late spring through mid-October.

Driving through this antiques shop–filled corner of Connecticut, you'll immediately notice three things: meandering roads, stone walls, and beautifully kept barns, their surrounding fields punctuated with contented-looking cows. Depending on the season, you may also notice a preponderance of khaki pants, blue button-down shirts, and navy blue blazers, for this area is home to several private boarding schools.

En route to **Woodstock,** a good place to base yourself for a tour, you'll drive through **North Woodstock** and past the photogenic **Red-White School** at the intersection of Routes 197 and 198. Don't watch for a red and white building, however, because the school is painted white with green trim. An 1873 one-room schoolhouse built on the site of an even earlier school building, which was painted red, the Red-White School is typical of the once-common New England schools in which several grades were taught by a single teacher. After serving generations of local residents, the Red-White School closed in 1939.

In Woodstock, you'll need no help spotting **Roseland Cottage,** an eye-popping, hot pink Gothic Revival home that dominates the village green. The 1846 "summer cottage" of Henry C. Bowen, a local resident who later moved to New York City and made a fortune in dry goods, the home retains much of its original furnishings and a carriage barn with its own bowling alley. Every attention to detail was paid within the home, right down to its hand-crafted doorknobs. The formal Victorian parterre garden remains planted just as it was when the Bowens inhabited the house during the warm summer months. Father of eleven children by two wives, Bowen spoke out on many important causes of his day, including abolition, temperance, and the importance of civic duty. He was a friend to many important people of his era, among them Presidents Rutherford B. Hayes, Benjamin Harrison, and Ulysses S. Grant, all of whom visited Roseland.

Woodstock is justifiably proud of its long history, and the **Woodstock Historical Society**'s impressive collection of items from the mid-1700s, including period clothing, household items, old maps, photographs, farm implements, and a signed letter from George Washington, is well worth a visit.

Roseland Cottage in Woodstock. Its gardens are filled with boxwood and other Victorian plantings.

If antiques call to you, you'll want to park the car and wander through the town's many antiques shops. In **Scranton's Shops** alone you'll find seven rooms full of quality antiques from several different dealers. Pace yourself, because this is only the beginning. Several other antiques shops will beckon as you continue your Quiet Corner tour.

For a snack or meal while you're in the area, try **Sweet Evalina's**, one of the Quiet Corner's most popular gathering spots. Another interesting option is to bring your own picnic to **Taylor Brooke Winery** in South Woodstock, where you can enjoy a glass of wine and your lunch right at the vineyard.

A marker tells the history of Woodstock.

County fairs have long played an important part in New England culture. In times gone by they were a way for farmers and farmers' wives to show off their prize cattle, crops, and handiwork and to relax after the busy planting and growing season. For more than 150 years, Woodstock has hosted the old-fashioned **Woodstock Fair**. The huge Woodstock Fairgrounds offer plenty of space for livestock and agricultural exhibits and a midway, plus fireworks, a parade, and musical acts. Children will be thrilled with the animals and the rides, to say nothing of a multitude of booths selling all things sticky, salty, deep-fried, and otherwise delectable.

If you're staying overnight in Woodstock, the **Inn at Woodstock Hill** has large rooms in a quiet setting. Its excellent dining room is a plus after a long day of driving. Or try the **Elias Child House Bed & Breakfast,** an 18th-century house in South Woodstock set amid lovely gardens.

Continue on Route 169 through Pomfret, whose first white settlers settled the town after purchasing land from Native Americans in 1686. Several mills once stood beside Pomfret's Mashamoquet Brook (*Mashamoquet* means "a stream for good fishing"), and here and there you can still spot the mill's foundations. **Mashamoquet Brook State Park** is a good stopping point for a stroll, a swim, or a picnic lunch. Pomfret is also home to the **Vanilla Bean Café,** with its well-deserved reputation for good food and welcoming atmosphere.

If antiques are still calling your name, plan a quick side trip onto Route 44 East and a long stop in **Putnam,** where shops like the **Antiques Marketplace** and **Jeremiah's** can keep you busy for hours. Both stores are packed with antiques from a variety of dealers, with an eclectic assortment at the Antiques Marketplace and a focus on glass and china at Jeremiah's. These are but two of the 17 or so antiques shops in Putnam.

WOLF DEN

The famous Revolutionary War hero General Israel Putnam is known, among other exploits, for having killed the last remaining wolf in Connecticut. After numerous homeowners' sheep and other farm animals were killed or maimed by the wolf, one snowy night in December 1742 Putnam tracked the animal for hours and ultimately dispatched it by crawling into its narrow den with a lighted flare and a musket. The den remains and can be visited in the area called Wolf Den within Mashamoquet State Park. (If you walk over to the den, take time to check out a couple of nearby rock formations that look surprisingly like a table and chair.) Putnam, who was born in what is now Danvers, Massachusetts, is best known for his participation in the Battle of Bunker Hill, where some scholars credit him with the famous command, "Don't fire till you see the whites of their eyes."

With this part of Connecticut still off many travelers' radar, Putnam remains peaceful and bucolic even in the peak summer months. The **Quinebog River** flows through town, there's usually plenty of parking, and bikers and walkers—the latter often with ice cream cones in hand—replace the heavy traffic and cacophony of many tourist destinations. With its solid brick buildings and leisurely ambiance, Putnam seems far more upbeat than many of New England's other former mill towns, which have struggled through hard times.

Leaving Putnam, head back to Route 169 South to **Brooklyn**. The large church on the village green is the first Unitarian church to be established in Connecticut and is typical of many plain and solid meetinghouses of its era. Built in 1771, the church's first minister, Rev. Samuel May, was an ardent abolitionist and supporter of women's rights. The **Unitarian Universalist Society in Brooklyn** still holds Sunday services here.

The nearby **Brooklyn Historic Society Museum** is worth a stop to learn more about the life and times of General Israel Putnam and about life in the early days of the town. The annual **Brooklyn Fair**, held in late August, is one of the oldest agricultural events in the country, with lots of old-fashioned exhibits and charm.

Try not to leave Brooklyn without at least one meal at the **Golden Lamb Buttery**, one of Connecticut's best-known restaurants. Housed in an old barn overlooking expansive fields and rolling hills, it's the perfect place for a special-occasion splurge.

Continue on to **Canterbury** to visit the **Prudence Crandall Museum**, dedicated to a remarkable woman who is the official state heroine of Connecticut. Born in 1803 to Quaker parents, Crandall was founder and administrator of the Canterbury Female Boarding School when she was approached in 1831 by a young black woman named Sarah Harris, who requested admission. Crandall enrolled her, touching off a firestorm of indignation among the parents of her white students. Parental dismay quickly turned to rudeness, insults, and anger, and parents pulled their daughters from the school, threatening to close it altogether. Undaunted, Crandall announced that the school would henceforth be devoted to the education of "young ladies and little misses of color." Seizing the opportunity, black students arrived from communities throughout New England. Connecticut promptly responded by passing a "Black Law" that made Crandall's school illegal. Ultimately she was arrested and briefly jailed, her

Frogs keep an eye on things in Willimantic.

case going before the courts three times before it was dismissed in 1834. Crandall reopened her school, but despite the support of several prominent abolitionists, including Rev. Samuel May of the Unitarian Universalist Society in nearby Brooklyn, this time taunts and anger escalated to outright violence and she was forced to close for good within two months. The state repealed the Black Law in 1838, but by then Crandall had moved to Kansas, where she remained until her death in 1890.

From Canterbury, turn west on Route 14 through Windham to **Willimantic**, the largest of the many former mill towns in northeastern Connecticut, for a quick look at the intriguing **Thread City Crossing Bridge**. From their perches atop enormous concrete spools of thread, four rather desultory-looking bronze frogs cast their beady gilt eyes over passersby. The bridge's name and the spools honor the mills of Willimantic, which in the mid-19th century churned out huge amounts of high-quality thread. The frogs, however, are another story. Supposedly, on a hot summer night in 1754 when the town was experiencing a drought, residents were awakened by a cacophony the likes of which they'd never heard before. Terrified citizens set out to see who or what might be attacking their town. To their surprise they came upon dozens—some versions of the story say hundreds—of dead bullfrogs that had apparently fought a battle to the end over a small pool of water, all that remained of an otherwise dried-up pond. The story has been carried down through the years and the frogs are now immortalized above the Willimantic River.

Fortunately, you won't have to suffer the frogs' thirst: the **Willimantic**

The Hale family homestead

Brewing Company offers microbrews from around New England in addition to its own excellent handcrafted brews—at least a dozen choices each month—and very good food all served up in a convenient downtown location.

Leaving Willimantic, head toward **Mansfield** on Route 32, where you'll find the **Mansfield Drive-in Theatre and Marketplace** at the junction of Routes 31 and 32. The drive-ins once so common across the country are dwindling now, down to about 400 from a high of 4,000 or more during the height of their popularity in the 1950s. If you're staying overnight in the Quiet Corner, this is inexpensive, nostalgic entertainment, complete with a playground for children, a snack bar stocked with old-fashioned treats, and movies that are always family-friendly. Prowling the Sunday flea market is fun for those with an itch to uncover a treasure or two.

From Mansfield, head north on Route 31 to Coventry. If it's time for lunch or dinner, you can relax at a table overlooking the river at the informal **Coventry Lake View Restaurant**. Coventry's **Daniel Rust House Bed & Breakfast** is an excellent overnight stopping point, especially for those interested in old houses. Ask to see the "secret closet" thought to be part of the Underground Railroad used by slaves escaping to the Northeast and Canada.

There's more history to be learned at the **Nathan Hale Homestead**, which memorializes the Revolutionary War hero who regretted that he had but one life to lose for his country. Captured as a spy by British troops and hanged in 1776, Hale never lived in the homestead, which was not built until the year he died. He was, however, born in a smaller house that once stood on the site. With its woods and fields and sturdy stone walls, the surrounding area is just the kind of setting in which one can envision a little boy growing up independent and strong. The grounds are beautiful, with herb and vegetable gardens and a corn maze open to the public in the fall. The focal point of a nearby cemetery at the intersection of Lake Street and Monument Hill Road is a tall monument to Hale, the official hero of Connecticut. He is not buried here, however, as no one ever learned what became of his body after the British hanged him from an apple tree in New York when he was just 21 years old.

Chances are, you will find it difficult to tear yourself away from the Quiet Corner, but when it's time to head back to Hartford, just return to Route 31 North and take Route 44 West.

IN THE AREA

Accommodations

Daniel Rust House Bed & Breakfast, 2011 Main Street, Coventry. Phone: 860-742-0032; www.thedanielrusthouse.com. This attractive old home has been welcoming travelers since 1800. Two acres of lovely grounds for walking. Inexpensive to moderate.

Elias Child House Bed & Breakfast, 50 Perrin Road, Woodstock. Phone: 1-877-974-9836; www.eliaschildhouse.com. A mid-18th-century home converted to a B&B with all the charm that fireplaces, porches, and well-tended gardens can bring. Hearty country breakfasts. Inexpensive.

Inn at Foxhill Farm, 760 Pomfret Street (Route 169), Pomfret. Phone: 860-928-5240; www.innatfoxhillfarm.com. A convenient, quiet B&B. Moderate.

Inn at Woodstock Hill, 94 Plaine Hill Road, Woodstock. Phone: 860-928-0528; www.woodstockhill.net. Twenty-one attractive rooms in a quiet setting. Excellent dining room. Continental breakfast included. Inexpensive to moderate.

Dining

Coventry Lakeview Restaurant, 50 Lake Street, Coventry. Phone: 860-498-0500; www.coventrylakeview.com. Enjoy a meal on the pretty deck overlooking the water or in the dining room. Open for lunch and dinner. Inexpensive.

Golden Lamb Buttery, 499 Wolf Den Road, Brooklyn. Phone: 860-774-4423; www.thegoldenlamb.com. Sip a pre-dinner drink on the deck or on a hayride around the property before settling in for a three-course prix-fixe dinner with several choices at each course. Jacket, tie, and reservations requested. Open spring through fall for lunch from Tues.–Sat., noon–2:30 and for dinner on Fri. and Sat. beginning at 7. Prix-fixe dinner, $75 per person.

Sweet Evalina's, 688 Route 169, Woodstock. Phone: 860-928-4029. Open 7–8 daily. Sandwiches, pizza, salads. Inexpensive.

Vanilla Bean Café, Route 169 at the intersection of Routes 44 and 97, Pomfret. Phone: 860-928-1562; www.thevanillabeancafe.com. Casual, popular spot with live entertainment. Open daily for breakfast (continental on weekdays; full breakfast on weekends), lunch, and dinner except closed for dinner on Mon. and Tues. Inexpensive.

Willimantic Brewing Co., 967 Main Street, Willimantic. Phone: 860-423-6777; www.willibrew.com. Beer, light meals, and friendly atmosphere. Open daily from 11:30 except Mon. from 4. Inexpensive.

Attractions and Recreation

Brooklyn Fair, 15 Fairgrounds Road, Brooklyn. Phone: 860-779-0012; www.brooklynfair.org. Held annually in late August. Parking $4; adult admission, $10; children 12 and under, free.

Brooklyn Historical Society Museum, Route 169, Brooklyn. Along with permanent displays chronicling the life of General Israel Putnam, the museum has changing exhibitions and artifacts from the town's past. Phone: 860-774-7728; www.brooklynct.org. Call for open hours. Free admission.

Mansfield Drive-in Theatre and Marketplace, Junction of Routes 31 and 32, Mansfield. Phone: 860-423-4441; www.mansfielddrivein.com. Flea market open Sun., 8–3, beginning in late March; movies begin weekends in early April and are shown nightly June–Aug. Call for open and closing dates. Flea market parking, $2. Site opens for movies at 7 PM; facilities include a snack bar and playground. Adults $9; children 4–11, $5; under 3, free. Every Wed., $18 per carload.

Mashamoquet Brook State Park, 147 Wolf Den Drive, Pomfret Center. Phone: 860-928-6121; http://ct.gov/dep/cwp/view.asp?a=2716&q =325238. Camping, grilling, and swimming facilities and good trails for walking and running. Open 8 AM to dusk. Small admission fee; additional fees for seasonal camping.

Nathan Hale Homestead, 2299 South Street, Coventry. Phone: 860-742-6917; http://ctlandmarks.org/index.php?page=nathan-hale-homestead. Contains family artifacts including a Bible belonging to Nathan Hale.

Open May–Oct. Call for opening and closing dates and times. Adults, $7; seniors and students, $6; under 6 free.

Prudence Crandall Museum, 1 South Canterbury Road (Junctions of Routes 14 and 169), Canterbury. Phone: 860-546-7800; http://ct.gov/CCT /cwp/view.asp?a=2127&q=302260. Open early May into the fall (call for exact dates and open hours). Adults $6; students and seniors, $4; children 5 and under, free.

Roseland Cottage, 556 Route 169, Woodstock. Phone: 860-928-4074; www.historicnewengland.org/historic-properties/homes/roseland-cottage /roseland-cottage. Open June 1–Oct. 15, Wed.–Sun. Tours given on the hour, 11–4. Adults, $8; seniors, $7; children 6–12, $4.

Taylor Brooke Winery, 848 Route 171, Woodstock. Phone: 860-974-1263; www.taylorbrookewinery.com. Wine tastings and picnic tables available. Open May–Dec., Fri. 11–6; Sat.–Sun., 11–5, and some holidays.

Unitarian Universalist Society in Brooklyn, Routes 6 and 169 at the Brooklyn Green, Brooklyn. Phone: 860-779-2623; http://home.mind spring.com/~apb2/UUSB/UUSB2.htm. Services are held every two weeks, April–Dec.; the congregation meets elsewhere during the winter months.

Woodstock Fair, 281 Route 169, Woodstock. Held Fri.–Mon. every Labor Day weekend. For information: www.woodstockfair.com.

Woodstock Historical Society, 523 Route 169, Woodstock. Phone: 860-928-1035; www.woodstockhistoricalsociety.org. Open Sun. from 12–4 and by appointment.

Shopping

Antiques Marketplace, 109 Main Street, Putnam. Phone: 860-928-0442; www.putnamantiques.com. A multidealer shop with a wide range of antiques. Call for open hours.

Jeremiah's Antiques Shops, 26 Front Street, Putnam. Phone: 860-963-2671; www.putnamantiques.com. A good variety of china and glass and other items. Call for open hours.

Scranton's Shops, 300 Route 169, South Woodstock. Phone: 860-728-3738. Antiques and collectibles. Open 11–5 daily except closed Tues.–Thurs. from Jan.–March.

Other Contacts

Woodstock information: www.townofwoodstock.com.

A tall clock on the waterfront across from the Herreshoff Museum quietly marks the passage of time.

CHAPTER

3

Rhode Island: East Bay and the Sakonnet Peninsula

Estimated length: About 14 miles from Providence to Warren; about 30 miles to tour the area.

Estimated time: Thirty minutes to get to Warren; a few hours to drive through the area, or longer to enjoy all there is to do.

Getting there: From Providence head east on I-195 to Route 114 (Exit 7), then go south on route 114 to Warren.

Highlights: Rich in history, Rhode Island's East Bay and Sakonnet Peninsula are a hidden treasure known mostly to adventurous visitors who travel beyond the better-known attractions of Newport and Providence. Come here to enjoy the gardens at the **Blithewold Mansion and Arboretum,** quiet paths for hiking and biking, historic mansions, even a contemporary vineyard—as well as the town of **Bristol,** which may be the most patriotic town in America, and the famous **Herreshoff Marine Museum.**

Originally called "Sowams" by the indigenous Wampanoag, **Warren** and the surrounding area has a long and interesting history. The Wampanoags' great sachem, Massasoit, who resided here, sold the land that now comprises Warren and nearby Barrington to settlers from the Plymouth Colony with whom he had formed a friendship that lasted throughout Massasoit's long life. Later, in the 18th century, Warren became the first home of Brown University (now located in Providence), and during the heyday of whaling and merchant ships, it was a major shipbuilding center. Today Warren is a quiet town of about eleven thousand residents.

Devotees of old houses may want to stop near the Warren waterfront to tour the **Maxwell House**, a gabled mid-18th-century home once owned by a minister and his seafaring sons. The house features unusual brickwork and a large central chimney. Rooms are furnished appropriately for the age of the house, now owned by the Massasoit Historical Association.

An interesting little shop for Rhode Island souvenirs, **Imagine** lives up to its name as a store full of unexpected treasures. Here you can buy Del's lemonade mix (don't leave Rhode Island without trying a fresh Del's lemonade, slushy and puckery with the taste of fresh lemons), and plenty of gifts for the folks back home. It's also an ice cream shop where you can bliss out on Rhode Island's favorite coffee ice cream. Rhode Islanders have an insatiable taste for all things coffee—in fact, the state's official drink is coffee milk, made with whole milk and a thick coffee syrup readily available in stores throughout the state.

From Warren, continue on Route 114 to **Bristol**. Republican or Democrat, conservative or liberal, you can't help but be charmed by Bristol, where maple and horse chestnut trees form a canopy above the streets of the self-styled most patriotic town in America. Even the dividing stripes down Route 114 in the town center are painted red, white, and blue, and by early May many storefronts and store windows are decked out in patriotic bunting and displays.

A visit here over the Fourth of July holiday is one you will always remember. For more than 125 years, Bristol has been home to the quintessential Independence Day parade, complete with floats and marching bands. The oldest continuous Fourth of July parade in the country takes two and a half to three hours to pass by. There are other events as well, including drum and bugle corps competitions and fireworks, often spread over several days, so be sure to check the schedule if your visit coincides with Bristol's favorite holiday.

For a look at what life was like in 18th-century Rhode Island, head for the living-history museum at **Coggeshall Farm**. It's easily reached by turning right off Route 114 onto Poppasquash Road and following the signs. Along with visiting the old farmhouse, blacksmith shop, and other outbuildings, visitors can wander through a kitchen garden and visit with the

Graceful Linden Place is in the heart of Bristol's historic section.

heirloom livestock in the fields. There's always something going on at the farm, from sheepshearing to maple sugaring.

There's a lot to see and do in Bristol, so you may want to take a break for lunch before continuing on. The **Lobster Pot** serves up lobsters and even a complete lobster and clam bake with all the fixings in a great location overlooking Narragansett Bay. Or, stop for a quick lunch at the **Bristol House of Pizza** to indulge in calzones, stromboli, grinders, or pizza.

When you're ready, continue on to **Linden Place** on Hope Street (Route 114), an 1810 Federal-style mansion that for six generations was home to the wealthy DeWolf and Colt families. Several US presidents were guests here, and actress Ethel Barrymore, who married into the family, was a frequent visitor. The place is sufficiently eye-popping to attract the attention of Hollywood filmmakers, who used it for several scenes in *The Great Gatsby.* The huge home at 500 Hope Street anchors the Bristol Historic District.

On the bucket list of many sailboat enthusiasts is a visit to the **Her-**

reshoff **Marine Museum** overlooking the Bristol waterfront. Between 1893 and 1934, the Herreshoffs built eight consecutive America's Cup winners while also producing boats for the US Navy. Along with more than 60 classic sailboats and yachts, the museum houses a model room, engines, photographs and other memorabilia, and the America's Cup Hall of Fame.

If you'd like to smell the roses, few gardens are more glorious than those at **Blithewold Mansion and Arboretum**, originally the summer estate of a Pennsylvania coal baron named Augustus Van Wickle. To reach Blithewold, head south on Route 114; the Blithewold is about a mile south of the Herreshoff Museum. Blithewold's 45-room mansion, built in 1908, has expansive views of Narragansett Bay and contains the family's original furnishings. Bequeathed to the public when the last family member died in 1976, the mansion provides an unusually detailed look at 19th-century life in an elegant New England summer home.

Augustus Van Wickle used Blithewold as a peaceful seaside retreat where he could escape from the pressures of his job, while his wife, Bessie, indulged her love of gardening. Apparently possessed of a keen eye as well as a green thumb, Bessie oversaw the planting of every garden and the construction of each structure on the estate's 33 acres. The Blithewold Arboretum has hundreds of species of rare and native trees. Nearly a mile of trails meander through the woods and gardens, allowing for comfortable walking even on the hottest summer day.

MOUNT HOPE FARM

If you have an interest in history or architecture, or just want a panoramic view of Mount Hope and Narraganset Bay, take Route 136 to Mount Hope Farm. Built in 1745 by wealthy Massachusetts resident Isaac Royall, the farmhouse has been added to many times over the centuries. As you stroll the 200 acres of woods and fields, you'll catch glimpses of wildlife and pass by a number of picturesque stone walls. The farm is located close to the site of the Wampanoags' headquarters during the bloody King Philip's War (1675–76), which occurred after the friendly relationship between colonists and Native Americans broke down following the death of Massasoit. It's also the place where King Philip—the name the English gave to Metacomet, son of Massasoit—was beheaded in 1676. A granite monument commemorating the war has been erected on one of the farm paths by the Rhode Island Historical Society. The grounds are open to the public for walking, jogging, and picnicking.

Fishing boats tie up for the afternoon in Bristol.

If you plan to stay overnight in the area, the **Bristol Harbor Inn** on the waterfront is convenient to downtown shops and restaurants. For sheer elegance, try **Point Pleasant Inn & Resort** on Poppasquash Point, a peninsula that juts into Narragansett Bay. The nucleus of the resort is a 33-room former mansion, now converted to elegant guest rooms. There is no lack of good places to eat in the evening in Bristol, among them the **DeWolf Tavern** in the casual setting of a renovated 1818 warehouse, a good place from which to watch the sun set over the water. **Le Central**, an unpretentious little bistro in the heart of town, serves excellent Mediterranean and French fare.

From Bristol, drive on to two quiet little towns on the Sakonnet peninsula where you'll almost feel your heart rate decrease and your blood pressure drop. Reach **Tiverton Four Corners** by crossing the Mount Hope Bridge into Portsmouth on Route 114. Turn left onto Boyd's Lane, then left again onto Anthony Road. After about a mile, turn onto Route 24/138 North and follow the signs to Route 77 South through Tiverton and into Tiverton Four Corners. It's a scenic drive beside the water, and Tiverton Four Corners itself is postcard-pretty with old stone walls and rolling hills.

A former stagecoach stop, the town gets its name from an early law that taverns could only be built at four-way intersections. Savvy area settlers made sure their town had such an intersection.

A National Historic District, Tiverton Four Corners has a number of 18th- and 19th-century homes that can be explored on a walking tour; a map can be downloaded from the town's website. One home on the route, the 1730 **Chase-Cory House**, is occasionally open to visitors, and the attractive 1846 A. P. White Store now houses **Provender**, where you can stop for sandwiches or a snack. And while in Tiverton Four Corners, don't pass up a chance to eat some of the best ice cream in the country at **Gray's Ice Cream**. A local institution since 1923, Gray's now boasts some 40 homemade flavors.

The peaceful lifestyle of a small town like Tiverton Four Corners

THE RIGHT STUFFIES

You'll see them everywhere, in restaurants large and small and even on the grill alongside hamburgers and hotdogs at backyard barbecues. Along with Del's lemonade, they're often the first choice of displaced Rhode Islanders returning home for a visit. They are stuffies, or stuffed clams—minced quahogs combined with breadcrumbs, onions, and garlic, and often ground chorizo, a type of spicy sausage. The mixture is stuffed back into the clamshell and baked or grilled. Bet you can't eat just one....

Sakonnet Vineyard in Little Compton

WHITHER THE WHIPPING POST?

From 1719 to 1812, a stone whipping post stood in what is now the parking lot for Gray's Ice Cream. Public floggings were legal and common during this period and included the whipping of women, who were punished severely for crimes like not following their husbands' orders. Whipping was outlawed in 1812, but the whipping post remained in the same spot until the 1950s when it disappeared overnight, never to be seen again. According to local lore, someone may have decided it would make a good front stoop or perhaps a group of women were simply tired of this reminder of the past and tore it down. Because the whipping post has never been identified as anyone's doorstep, rumor has it that the perpetrators buried it and a few older women in Tiverton Four Corners know where. But they're not telling, and the mystery of the missing whipping post continues....

attracts artisans whose galleries offer good opportunities for shopping. You'll find beautifully woven items for the home at the gallery of **Amy C. Lund, Handweaver,** and the work of other artisans from across the country at **Courtyards,** both located on Main Road. Nearby, **Four Corners Grille** is a popular informal eatery.

End your tour by taking Route 77 from Tiverton Four Corners to Little Compton. If you enjoy wine, plan a stop at tranquil **Sakonnet Vineyards** off Route 77 South, where visitors are welcome for tours and wine tastings. Wines from the 50-acre vineyard have won a number of well-deserved awards. More than 35 years ago when the vineyard was established, Rhode Island may not have struck many as a prime location for growing grapes. Sakonnet Vineyards has proved naysayers wrong by producing a variety of excellent wines including a flavorful gewürztraminer, a well-balanced pinot noir, the vineyard's own hybrid vidal blanc, and a sparkling wine made in the traditional *méthode champenoise* to enjoy while stargazing on a hot summer evening.

Be sure to check out Little Compton's charming town common— watch for the signs—the only one in Rhode Island. Surrounded by houses, small shops, and a neat little local

MONUMENT TO A CHICKEN

The Adamsville section of Little Compton is the birthplace of the Rhode Island Red hen, a sturdy breed that lays the brown eggs popular throughout New England. What is believed to be the country's only monument to a chicken can be seen near the ballfield. The Rhode Island Red has been further honored by being named the official state bird.

SHINING A LIGHT ON EAST BAY

Several lighthouses dot the shoreline in this part of Rhode Island. In Bristol, Hog Island Shoal Light marks the entrance to the harbor. Now privately owned, it is still an active light. Near the south end of Mount Hope Bridge is the inactive Bristol Ferry Light, now a private residence. The Prudence Island Ferry from Bristol brings visitors to the site of Prudence Island Light. The oldest lighthouse in Rhode Island and still an active aid to navigation, it is noted for the unusual "birdcage" railings protecting the light. At the end of Route 77 off Sakonnet Point in Little Compton there's a clear view of active Sakonnet Point Light.

restaurant called **Commons Lunch**, the whole area is on the National Register of Historic Places. Stretch your legs with a walk through the common and enjoy the feeling of stepping back to a quieter time.

Continue south on Route 77 to Sakonnet Point. Elaborate homes share the point with a commercial wharf where rugged fishermen gather and trucks rumble in and out, driving their catch to market. Surf crashes against the breakwater, and sport fishermen try their luck off the rocks. You may be so charmed by the whole scene that you'll want to stay in Little Compton for a day or so. One of the town's little B&Bs may fill the bill. Try **Harmony Home Farm** or the **Edith Pearl Bed & Breakfast**, both in interesting historic homes.

It may be hard to tear yourself away from this quiet corner of Rhode Island, but when you must, head north on Route 77 to retrace your trip back to Providence.

IN THE AREA

Accommodations

Bristol Harbor Inn, 259 Thames Street, Bristol. Phone: 1-866-254-1444; www.bristolharborinn.com. Inexpensive to moderate, continental breakfast included.

Edith Pearl Bed & Breakfast, 250 West Main Road (Route 77), Little Compton. Phone: 401-592-0053; www.edithpearl.com. Some rooms with shared baths. Moderate; breakfast included.

The breakwater and commercial fishing wharf at Sakonnet Point

Harmony Home Farm, 456 Long Highway, Little Compton. Phone: 401-635-2283; www.harmonyhomefarm.com. Inexpensive to moderate; continental breakfast included.

Point Pleasant Inn & Resort, 333 Poppasquash Point, Bristol. Phone: 401-253-0627; www.pointpleasantinn.com. To celebrate a special occasion, or if you've always had a longing to experience the elegance of life in an English manor, this just may be the spot. Rates include, among many other perks, a full breakfast, snacks, afternoon tea, open bar, cheese and fruit, desserts and cordials, laundry, and resort amenities ranging from a pool to boccie and use of the fitness center. Very expensive.

Dining

Bristol House of Pizza, 55 State Street. Phone: 401-253-2550; www.bristolhouseofpizza.com. Inexpensive.

Commons Lunch, 48 Commons, Little Compton. Phone: 401-635-4388. New England fare, including chowders and Rhode Island specialties. Open for breakfast, lunch, and dinner. Inexpensive.

DeWolf Tavern, 259 Thames Street, Bristol. Phone: 401-254-2005; www.dewolftavern.com. Restaurant open daily for dinner; tavern open daily for lunch. Moderate.

Four Corners Grille, 3841 Main Road, Tiverton Four Corners. Phone: 401-624-1510. Open for lunch and dinner. Inexpensive.

Gray's Ice Cream, 16 East Road, Tiverton Four Corners. Phone: 401-624-4500; www.graysicecream.com. All kinds of ice cream treats. Inexpensive.

Le Central, 483 Hope Street (Route 114), Bristol. Phone: 401-396-9965; www.lecentralbristol.net. Great French food and a good wine list. Open daily for lunch and dinner; Sunday brunch. Tapas weeknights to 6:30. Moderate.

Lobster Pot, 119 Hope Street (Route 114), Bristol. Phone; 401-253-9100; www.lobsterpotri.com. A local favorite since 1929. Open daily for lunch and dinner. Inexpensive to moderate.

Provender, 3883 Main Road, Tiverton Four Corners. Phone: 401-624-8084. Sandwiches, soups, muffins, and snacks in an informal setting. Open daily to 5 PM. Inexpensive.

Attractions and Recreation

Blithewold Mansion and Arboretum, 101 Ferry Road (Route 114), Bristol. Phone: 401-253-2707; www.blithewold.org. Gardens and mansion open from mid-Apr. to mid-Oct. from Wed.–Sun. and on most Mon. holidays. Also open in Dec. for monthlong "Christmas at Blithewold." Admission: Adults, $10; seniors and students, $8; ages 6–17, $2; ages 5 and under, free.

Chase-Cory House, 3908 Main Road, Tiverton. This Cape-style house with a gambrel roof is usually open from May–Sept., Sun. 2–4:30.

Coggeshall Farm, Poppasquash Road (off Route 114), Bristol. Phone: 401-253-9062; www.coggeshallfarm.org. Tour the buildings and outbuildings and enjoy visits with the livestock. Many special events throughout the year, including a maple-sugaring weekend and a harvest fair. Open Tues.–Sun., 10–4. Adults, $3; children, $2.

Herreshoff Marine Museum/America's Cup Hall of Fame, 1 Burnside Street (off Route 114), Bristol. Phone: 401-253-5000; www.herreshoff .org. Open daily, 10–5. Adults, $8; seniors, $7; students and children 11–17, $4; under 10, free.

Linden Place, 500 Hope Street, Bristol. Phone: 401-253-0390; www .lindenplace.org. Open early May through Columbus Day. Tours Sat. 10–4 and sometimes on Sun.; call to confirm. Admission fee charged.

Maxwell House, 59 Church Street, Warren. www.massasoithistorical.org. Check website for special events such as teas and 18th-century dinners. Tours offered Sat. 10–2. Admission free.

Mount Hope Farm, 250 Metacom Avenue (Route 136), Bristol. Phone: 401-254-1745; www.mounthopefarm.com.

Prudence Island Ferry, Church Street Wharf, Bristol. Phone: 401-253-9808; www.prudenceferry.com. Regular trips throughout the year to little Prudence Island, home to fewer than 100 residents and location of Prudence Island Light. Call or check website for schedule. Adult round-trip, $6.20; child, $2.10.

Sakonnet Vineyards, 162 West Main Road, Little Compton. Phone: 1-800-919-4637; www.sakonnetwine.com. Open year-round; call for open hours.

Shopping

Amy C. Lund, Handweaver, 3879 Main Road, Tiverton Four Corners. Phone: 401-816-0000; www.amyclundhandweaver.com. Open Wed.–Sun.

Courtyards, 3980 Maine Road, Tiverton Four Corners. Phone: 401-624-8682; www.courtyardsltd.com. Open daily except Mon.

Imagine, 3 Miller Street, Warren. Phone: 401-245-4200; imaginegift stores.com. A funky building and an eclectic assortment of gifts make this an interesting stop.

Other Contacts

Bristol Fourth of July Celebration: www.july4thbristolri.com.

Tiverton Four Corners information: www.tivertonfourcorners.com.

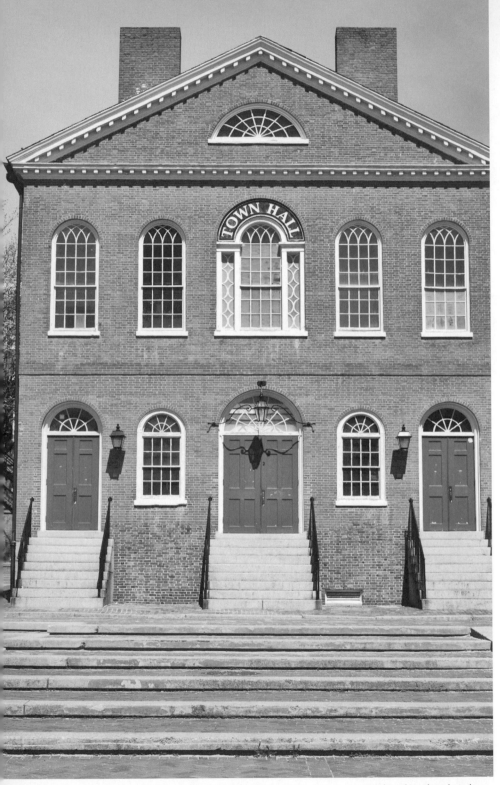

The Old Town Hall in Salem, built 1816–17, is a fine example of Federal style.

Massachusetts: The North Shore

Estimated length: About 22 miles from Boston to Danvers and 55 miles to tour the area.

Estimated time: About a half hour from Boston to Danvers. To explore the towns and enjoy the beaches, a weekend is perfect, although you can also drive the route in a day or less.

Getting there: Take Route 1 North from Boston to Danvers, then Route 62 East for about 2 miles, and turn right onto Maple Street. Then turn right onto Hobart Street to the Witchcraft Victims' Memorial on the left.

Highlights: In many ways, Boston's North Shore is a microcosm of all that is good about New England. Perhaps it's the area's intriguing history or its location—quiet, near the sea, yet close to the bright lights of Boston— that make the North Shore so appealing. Whatever the reason, residents here are among the happiest and friendliest you will meet anywhere. Whether your interests lie in history, architecture, beachcombing, boating, hiking, antiques, or art, you will find plenty to do. The **Rebecca Nurse Homestead** remains much as it was when its unfortunate occupant was accused of witchcraft, the **Peabody Essex Museum** attracts travelers from all over the world, and the **McIntire Historic District** includes one of the most architecturally beautiful streets in the country.

The Rebecca Nurse Homestead in Danvers

Winters are quiet, but many historical attractions remain open, restaurants and hotels run cost-saving specials, and historic homes are beautifully decorated for the holidays. Springtime can be lovely, with ancient lilacs in bloom, miles of deserted beaches to enjoy, and first pick of the antiques that shop owners have accumulated over the winter. Summer visitors enjoy long walks along some of the country's most architecturally stunning streets, the best swimming on white-sand beaches, fried clams in **Essex,** where they were invented, old-fashioned Fourth of July celebrations, and festivals galore. Fall brings crisp, cool nights, apples to pick, and harvest fairs to enjoy. And of course in late October thousands of travelers arrive in **Salem,** some for lengthy visits and others for just a short spell....

Salem has long promoted itself as "Witch City," but the story of the 1692 witchcraft hysteria really begins in **Danvers,** now a town of about 25,000 residents that was then known as Salem Village. In the late 17th century, Salem Village was mostly scattered farms and rolling countryside, but the pastoral area did have an active meetinghouse to which the Reverend Samuel Parris came in 1689 along with his wife and children. Two slaves, Tituba and John Indian, whom Parris had acquired in Barbados, also accompanied them. The newcomers' arrival set the stage for one of the most infamous events in American history.

What caused the fits and frenzy and claims of being bewitched among several young girls in the village—starting with Parris's own daughter and his niece, who had come to live with them—may never be known. Scholars have attributed their seizures and tremors to a variety of causes, including Tituba's dark voodoo tales, bread mold that might have caused hallucinations, and even teenage angst. Whatever the reason, before long the girls began accusing a number of people—most of them elderly and debilitated—of witchcraft. Ultimately 14 women and 5 men were hanged, and one man was crushed to death, while dozens of others languished in jail.

Danvers has always remained low-key about its role in the witchcraft era, but the town quietly maintains several related historical sites and markers. **The Witchcraft Victims' Memorial** is located at 176 Hobart Street. The monument lists the names of all who died during the hysteria along with poignant statements made at their trials. Just beyond the memorial, on the corner of Hobart and Centre streets, is the site of the meetinghouse where the Reverend Parris preached. A Congregational church now stands there along with an historic marker.

The Samuel Parris Archaeological Dig has unearthed the foundation of the 1681 village parsonage. It was here, a few years later, that Tituba spun the stories that may have titillated the imaginations of impressionable village girls. There is no parking area, so park on Hobart Street and, turning right onto Centre Street, walk about 200 yards to the cart path that leads to the site. To get a feel for what it must have been like during those dark

---

THE PUTNAM HOUSE

In addition to the famous Rebecca Nurse Homestead, about a dozen other homes in Danvers exist from the witchcraft era, including the **Putnam House** at 438 Maple Street, the town's main street. Built around 1648, in 1692 the house belonged to Joseph Putnam, uncle of one of the young women who claimed to be bewitched and one of the few citizens brave enough to call the whole thing nonsense. Legend has it that, in anticipation of being accused of witchcraft and hauled off to jail himself, Putnam kept a loaded gun and a fast horse at the ready. Twelve generations of the family lived in the Putnam House, including General Israel Putnam, commander at the Battle of Bunker Hill, who was born in the house in 1718. Today the home is owned by the Danvers Historical Society.

---

days so long ago, walk slowly along the short cart path and into the clearing, where interpretive markers explain the history of the house, which was torn down in 1784.

Before you leave this section of Danvers, you may want to check out two points of interest unrelated to the witchcraft delusion but historically interesting. Leaving Hobart Street, turn right onto Centre Street and drive about a quarter of a mile to the **Village Training Field** at the corner of Centre and Ingersoll streets. Citizens of Salem Village held military drills here as early as 1671 and Minutemen marched from here to the Battle of Lexington and Concord in 1775, suffering heavy losses. Continue down Ingersoll Street to visit early-19th-century **Glen Magna,** originally the luxurious estate of Joseph Peabody, the wealthiest shipping merchant in Salem. Wander the tranquil grounds or take a guided tour of the home built in Colonial Revival style. Surrounding the estate, a town-owned park with walking trails makes a pleasant place to take a break from driving.

Perhaps the most famous site from the witchcraft era is the **Rebecca Nurse Homestead**. Built around 1678, it was the home of Francis Nurse and his elderly wife. At the height of the hysteria, frail Rebecca was accused of practicing witchcraft, taken from her bedroom, tried, and despite testimony from some 40 of her neighbors who spoke of her unblemished character, hanged in July 1692. To get there from the Village Training Field, turn left onto Centre Street and after 0.5 mile, bear left onto Holten Street. Travel about 0.5 mile to the traffic light at Pine Street and turn right onto the narrow lane leading to the Rebecca Nurse homestead. The Nurse property has been used in several documentaries and films, including Alistair Cooke's *America* and *Three Sovereigns for Sarah.*

When you're ready for a break in your travels, Danvers has several excellent restaurants, including casual **Sam and Joe's Cafe,** a longtime local favorite with terrific pizza, and the elegant **Danvers Yacht Club,** both in the Danversport area. If you'd like to stay overnight, the **Crowne Plaza Boston North Shore** has excellent amenities in a convenient location for touring the area.

SORRY, GEORGE

Danvers separated from Salem Village in 1752, an act that didn't sit well with King George III, who tried to rescind the uppity colonists' decision by issuing a decree stating, "The King Unwilling." In what may have been the ultimate snub, Danvers citizens incorporated his words into the Town Seal, where they remain today.

THE BEST OF BOSTON

The hub of New England, Boston lies on neither a back road nor a byway. But because many travelers begin their New England journeys by flying into Logan Airport or driving into the city, a few words about "Beantown" may be helpful. If you arrive in Boston by car or rent one after you arrive in the city, park at your hotel for the duration and either take public transportation or walk. Driving Boston's crowded, twisty streets is not for the faint of heart.

If your time in Boston is brief, consider these highlights that make the city unique.

1. **The Freedom Trail**. American history comes alive as you follow the 2.5-mile red brick trail past Paul Revere's House, the Old North Church, Faneuil Hall, the Granary Burying Ground, and a dozen other historic sites. Walk the trail on your own or take a tour from the Boston Common Visitors' Information Center. Guides in colonial garb regale visitors with anecdotes, both humorous and historical. Contact: www.thefreedomtrail.org. Ninety-minute tours: Adults, $12; students and seniors, $10; children, $6.

2. **Boston Common** and **Boston Public Garden**. The country's oldest public park, Boston Common's 50 acres were once set aside for cattle grazing and public hangings. On any given day you may see a political rally, a soapbox speaker, a protest march, or a church group reaching out to the homeless. Nannies push strollers, office workers eat lunch on park benches, joggers hurry by, and camera-toting tourists photograph the park's historic statues and the colorful goings-on. The Common, as it's always referred to, is a stop on the Freedom Trail. Contact: www.cityofboston.gov/FreedomTrail/boston common.asp.

   The oldest public botanical garden in the country, Boston Public Garden was laid out in 1837 near the Common; both are part of a series of parks known as Boston's Emerald Necklace. Boston Public Garden's splashy, Victorian-themed plantings include some 80 species of flowers and trees. Pedal-powered Swan Boats, owned by the same family for more than 130 years, sail on the park's lagoon from mid-April to mid- September. A languid 15-minute ride on the paddleboats in this tranquil heart of the city is a memorable experience. Contact: (Boston Public Garden) www.cityofboston.gov /parks/emerald/Public_Garden.asp; (Swan Boats) www.swanboats.com. Swan Boat fares: Adults, $2.75; seniors, $2; children ages 2–15, $1.50.

3. **Museums.** In a city noted for its museums, these are standouts:
   The Museum of Fine Arts, one of the country's largest and finest. Contact: www.mfa.org. Adults, $20; seniors and students 18 and over, $18; chil-

dren 6 and under, free. Youth 7–17, $7.50 except free after 3 PM weekdays and all weekend.

The Museum of Science, a hands-on museum for adults and children alike. Contact: www.mos.org. Adults, $20; seniors, $18; children 3–11, $17.

The Institute of Contemporary Art, including modern art in all media. Contact: www.icaboston.org. Adults, $15; seniors, 13; students $10; ages 17 and under, free.

The Isabella Stewart Gardner Museum, fascinating visitors since 1924, when its founder left her extensive art collection and home to the city with the proviso that nothing ever be changed. Her wishes have been respected, even following one of the art world's most stunning thefts in 1990 when works by Rembrandt, Degas, and Vermeer were removed or cut from their frames. Empty frames and faded spots on the walls remain. Contact: www.gardnermuseum.org. Adults, $12; seniors, $10; college students, $5; children 18 and under free with adult; anyone named Isabella, always free.

4. **The North End.** The historic Italian district bustles with festivals and fun throughout the year. Restaurants range from pasta places to fine dining establishments; for dessert it's a gelato or cannoli from one of the small shops along Hanover Street.

5. **Fenway Park.** America's oldest baseball stadium and home to the Boston Red Sox and "Red Sox Nation," that group of fans known for their baseball savvy and fierce loyalty. Evenings at Fenway are part sports event, part soap opera, part people-watching extravaganza, and thoroughly unforgettable. If you can't snag tickets, consider a tour of the park and the legendary "Green Monstah." Yankees hats are best left in your luggage. For schedules, tickets, and tours contact: www.boston.redsox.mlb.com/bos/ballpark/tour.jsp. Tours: Adults, $12; seniors, $11; children 3–15, $10.

Boston has great hotels, and is acclaimed as one of the country's top foodie cities. For old Boston elegance without attitude, try the **Fairmont Copley Plaza** (www.fairmont.com/copleyplaza), where hotel guests can walk black Labrador mascot Catie Copley. The popular **Oak Bar** serves classic cocktails. The ultra-modern **Fairmont Battery Wharf** (www.fairmont.com/batterywharf) near the harbor and the historic North End is a gem.

The **Bristol Lounge** at the luxurious **Four Seasons Hotel** (www.fourseasons .com/boston) has won well-deserved culinary awards. A charming afternoon tea is served overlooking the Boston Public Garden.

Any rumors you've heard about solemn New Englanders will fade away at the lively **Liberty Hotel** (www.libertyhotel.com), located in what was once the Charles Street Jail. An informal restaurant is called **Clink**; a larger restaurant is **Scampo**

(Italian for "escape"), both with excellent food. Drink up at **Alibi Bar**. And so on.

Other popular eateries include Boston's oldest, the **Union Oyster House** (www.unionoysterhouse.com) for excellent seafood, and **Hamersley's Bistro** (www.hamersleysbistro.com), noted for cassoulet and for their signature chicken with garlic and lemon.

Salem lies just five miles from Danvers. To get there from the Rebecca Nurse Homestead, drive out of the property and turn right onto Pine Street, then right onto Sylvan Street, left onto Route 114, and continue into Salem. A good first stop is the **National Park Service Regional Visitor Center** downtown, where you can take inexpensive ranger-led tours and pick up maps and information about Salem and nearby towns. A free orientation film provides a good overview.

Along with its witch history, Salem has a long literary heritage and an impressive maritime tradition that is just now receiving the attention it deserves. To get almost anywhere in Salem, however, you'll first have to wend your way past stores filled with witch kitsch like warty-nosed witch magnets and bumper stickers proclaiming, "My Other Vehicle is a Broom." It's all done in good humor, and visiting children and teens find the mix of serious history and commercialized hysteria especially appealing.

History buffs can get the most authentic look at Salem's role in the events of 1692 by visiting the **Witch House**. Actually the home of Judge Jonathan Corwin, this is the only remaining Salem building that played a role in the witchcraft era. It was Corwin who conducted examinations of the accused and served on the court that ultimately condemned 19 to death. A stop at the **Salem Witch Museum,** the best of the many commercial attractions related to the witchcraft era, gives an overview of the victims, the trials, and the events that led up to them.

After exploring the Witch House and Salem Witch Museum, it may be time for a break. Try **Red's Sandwich Shop,** where you can grab a coffee or have breakfast or lunch. History oozes from the very walls at Red's, housed in a building that in the 1700s was the Old London Coffeehouse.

Salem is a popular stop in any season, but never more so than in the month of October. An event called **Haunted Happenings** brings as many as ninety thousand visitors to the city for everything from plays and readings to a costume party at the venerable **Hawthorne Hotel**. Advance (*way* in advance) reservations are a must for room reservations in October, but at other times of year the hotel makes a great base for exploring the North

Shore. **Nathaniel's**, the hotel's formal restaurant, and the informal **Tavern,** popular with locals, are both good choices for meals.

The hotel's name and restaurant are a nod to one of Salem's most famous citizens, author Nathaniel Hawthorne, who was born here on July 4, 1804. In the 1950s the house in which he was born was moved from a few streets away to the grounds of the Ingersoll-Turner mansion, which Hawthorne immortalized as the **House of the Seven Gables**. This remarkable 17th-century wooden mansion that inspired a novel has a hidden staircase and is filled with period furniture.

Nearby you'll find the **National Park Service Salem Maritime National Historic Site,** and it is here that you'll get a glimpse of the maritime powerhouse that once was Salem. In the harbor are remnants of three wharves, a poignant reminder of a time when this was one of the country's busiest ports. The **Derby Wharf Light Station** at the tip of Derby Wharf is one of just a handful of similar square-shaped lighthouses in the country. Berthed at Derby Wharf is a replica of *Friendship,* a late-18th-century tall ship that sailed around the world 15 times, returning with exotic goods and spices, until it was captured by the British during the War of 1812. The **Derby House,** home to America's first millionaire, is just across the street from the wharves. Many other Salem families had also made their fortunes by the time clipper ships became too large for Salem's harbor, after which its importance as a port quickly diminished.

Along the waterfront you'll also find Pickering Wharf, a mix of small shops, restaurants, and condominiums. Try the **Antiques Gallery,** where some 40 dealers display their wares, or **Cat 'n' the Fiddle,** for souvenirs and retro gifts.

The legacy of those years when Salem's ships sailed to China and elsewhere, returning laden with wondrous items from the East, lives on at the **Peabody Essex Museum**. Originally founded by ships' captains to display the riches they brought back from their travels, today the museum's collection totals nearly one million works, and its Asia collection is internationally famous. One of the most unusual sights at the museum is the Yin Yu Tang house, originally the multigeneration home of one family in southeastern China. Dismantled, shipped, and fully reassembled at the museum, the extraordinary home looks as if the family just stepped out for a moment.

Before leaving Salem, walk or drive along some of the most remarkable streets in the country, famous for the beauty of their architecture and their historical importance. In the downtown area, the **McIntire Historic District** comprises Broad, Federal, Cambridge, and Chestnut streets, location of some three hundred historic homes built between the mid-17th and the early 20th centuries. Most are privately owned and not open to the public. A 1-mile walking trail is marked with plaques stamped with a sheaf of wheat, a symbol often used by renowned Salem architect Samuel McIntire, for whom the district is named. Several McIntire-designed buildings can be found along the trail. If time is limited, at least try to visit Chestnut Street, acclaimed as one of the most beautiful streets in America. **Hamilton Hall,** at 9 Chestnut Street, is considered a McIntire masterpiece, with no detail left to chance. What look like wrought iron decorations outside the building are actually supports for springs beneath the second-floor ballroom, put in place so that women could dance all night without their feet growing tired. The handsome building is still used for weddings and other gatherings.

If these lovely old houses have caught your attention, you can stay overnight in a charming 1845 Greek Revival house, the **Amelia Payson House,** a bed & breakfast inn in the heart of downtown Salem from which you can walk to just about everything.

From Salem, take Route 1A toward Beverly, then turn right onto scenic Route 127, which winds through the North Shore seaside communities of Monteserrat, Pride's Crossing, and Beverly Farms and into the area known as Massachusetts' "Other Cape." Far smaller and less well known than Cape Cod, **Cape Ann** includes the towns of Manchester-by-the-Sea, Gloucester, Essex, and Rockport, each with a distinctive personality.

THE SPIRIT OF '76

The North Shore town of Marblehead lies off Route 114, about 4 miles from Salem. Here you can visit both the beautiful harbor that has given Marblehead fame as one of the world's yachting capitals and the famous Archibald Williams painting, *The Spirit of '76*. The patriotic painting of two men playing the fife and drum accompanied by a young drummer boy was first exhibited at the 1876 Centennial Exposition in Philadelphia. How did a painting by an Ohio artist, first exhibited in Pennsylvania, end up in a small North Shore town? It seems that Henry Devereaux, the model for the drummer boy, was the son of General Devereaux, a prominent Marblehead citizen. After the painting captured the country's imagination following the exposition and a national tour, the general purchased it for his hometown. The painting hangs in the Selectmen's Room at Abbott Hall at 188 Washington Street, where the public is welcome to view it.

Singing Beach in Manchester-by-the-Sea

Quaint **Manchester-by-the-Sea** is known for its photogenic clapboard houses weathered by years of exposure to the salt air. Here you'll find a little jewel of a beach where the sand squeaks musically as you walk or run on it. **Singing Beach** is open all year with lovely views that make a stop worthwhile. To get there, follow Route 127 to the intersection with the Post Office. Route 127 makes a sharp left turn here. Instead of turning, head straight over the railroad tracks onto Beach Street and continue about 0.5 mile to the beach.

After enjoying some beach time, return to Route 127 and continue toward **Gloucester** (pronounce it GLOSS-tah if you don't want to be immediately identified as a tourist), first stopping at beautiful **Stage Fort Park,** which looks out over Gloucester Harbor. In 1623 settlers arrived in this area from Plymouth; later, a fort stood here to defend the town against the British. You may want to stop for a walk, a swim, or picnic, or to observe **Eastern Point Light** and **Ten Pound Island Light**, two typical New England lighthouses. Neither is open to the public, alas. A branch of the **Gloucester Visitors' Center** is located at the park.

Gloucester is the oldest seaport in the United States, and the place from which some ten thousand fishermen have set sail, never to return. Those lost at sea are remembered at the often-photographed bronze **Gloucester Fisherman's Memorial** on Stacy Boulevard. Nearby, another memorial pays tribute to wives and children left behind.

To see for yourself what it was like to sail on the schooners that once headed to the Grand Banks fishing grounds, sign up for a 2-hour sail on the **Schooner *Thomas E. Lannon,*** a replica built in nearby Essex. You can pitch in and help hoist the sails or just sit back and supervise. Gloucester is also a great spot for whale-watching trips. Naturalists accompanying trips aboard cruises run by **7 Seas Whale Watch** can tell you everything you've ever wanted to know about whales, their habitat, and other wildlife you may spot along the way.

Art lovers visiting Gloucester during the warm-weather months will enjoy the **Rocky Neck Art Colony,** thought to be the oldest working art colony in the country. Childe Hassam, Fitz Henry Lane, Mark Rothko, and many others painted here.

And if you're in Gloucester during the dinner hour or on Sunday, try **Elliott's at the Blackburn** near the waterfront. The chef is from Gloucester, and the all-American cuisine takes advantage of local seafood. A lively jazz brunch begins late on Sunday mornings and continues throughout much of the day.

From Gloucester continue about 4 miles on Route 127 to scenic little **Rockport,** where the red fishing shack known as **Motif #1** has enchanted and inspired artists and photographers since 1884. The original fish house was completely destroyed during a 1978 blizzard, but the rebuilt shack is still among the most photographed and painted scenes in the country. You'll find Motif #1 on Bradley Wharf near **Bearskin Neck,** an enclave of art galleries, restaurants, and small shops selling paintings, pottery, jewelry, and souvenirs. Try the **Rockport Fudgery** for sweets, and **Bearskin Neck Leathers** for a wide variety of leather goods.

From Bearskin Neck (named for wild bears that once roamed there), lighthouse enthusiasts can see **Straightsmouth Island Light** (not open to the public). On Thacher Island off Rockport are the twin lighthouses of **Cape Ann Light Station**, which can be visited by guided boat tours in summer. Built in 1771, these are the only operating twin lighthouses in the United States and have been designated a National Historic Landmark. One tower is open for visitors, with spectacular views from the top. Depending on when you come, you may see nests full of eggs or recently hatched birds; the quiet island is a prime nesting site for gulls.

Rockport can be a peaceful place to spend the night before visiting the final destinations on your tour. The historic **Emerson Inn by the Sea** has a quiet ambiance and an award-winning restaurant.

THEY THAT GO
DOWN TO THE SEA
IN SHIPS
⚓ ⚓ ⚓
1623 — 1923

The 8-ft.-tall statue of a fisherman celebrates Gloucester's ties to the sea.

Leaving Rockport, continue on Route 127 until it ends at a traffic circle (called a rotary in much of New England). Take the first exit off the traffic circle (Route 128 South), then take the Route 133 exit toward **Essex,** where you'll want to fuel up on the famous Essex fried clams before settling in for a day of exploring or antiquing. Way back in 1916 a man named "Chubby" Woodman dropped a clam into a pot of bubbling oil and started an enduring American institution. **Woodman's** is completely informal—order at a window, wait for your number to be called, pick up your food, and eat at rustic picnic benches. This is the essence of dining near the sea, where the clams were probably still burrowing in the sand a few hours before they were heaped on your plate, and the lobster was caught that morning. Midsummer lines can be long, but the reward is a huge platter of tasty seafood.

Essex was a shipbuilding center for more than three hundred years, and saw the construction of more two-masted wooden fishing vessels than any other town in the world. The story of how such a tiny village became a major shipbuilding stronghold is well told at the **Essex Shipbuilding Museum.** More than eight thousand items related to Essex boatbuilding offer insight into how the ships were built and the tools used to construct them.

Most serious collectors of antiques have Essex on their radar, and with good reason. More than 35 antiques shops (and, yes, a handful of junque stores) line Route 133 as it passes through town. Most are within walking distance of each other. For fine American antiques, try the appropriately named **Americana Antiques,** a fixture in the heart of Main Street for more than 40 years.

Leaving Essex and Cape Ann, travel along Route 133 to **Ipswich.** If you are interested in period homes, you'll be enchanted with Ipswich, which has more houses dating from the First Period—the years between 1625 and 1725—than any other town in the country. Many are located on and around County Street. Watch for wonderful old architectural details

THE BEACH WITH THE BIG NAME

Less well known to visitors than other North Shore beaches, **Wingaersheek Beach,** with its powdery white sand and tidal pools, has long been popular with locals. Stop for a swim or kick off your shoes and go exploring for shells and hermit crabs and know that you are relaxing where Ralph Waldo Emerson once found inspiration while living close to the water. As for that unusual name? It may have come from a Native American word, but no one seems to know for sure. To reach Wingaersheek, in Gloucester, take Exit 13 off Route 128, then take Concord Street to Atlantic Avenue.

Small shops at Bearskin Neck in Rockport

such as bull's-eye windows, Indian shutters, and unusually designed doors. If you're serious about old houses, stop first at the **Ipswich Visitor Information Center** on South Main Street for a walking-tour brochure that highlights many of the most important homes.

There has always been good-natured rivalry between Essex and Ipswich for bragging rights as the nation's Fried Clam Capital. One of Woodman's rivals is the funky **Clam Box** in Ipswich, an example of form following function if ever there was one. The restaurant looks exactly like a giant clam box, so get your camera out to record your visit and then step inside to do your own culinary critique.

Before heading back to Boston, stop at **Crane Beach** for a swim and a walk along 4.5 miles of sparkling white sand or a hike through 7 miles of trails through the dunes. The beach is part of the large Crane Estate complex. Near the water, a 59-room mansion called **Castle Hill**, once a millionaire's summer "cottage," is now a National Historic Landmark.

Leaving Ipswich to return to Boston, continue on Route 133 to Route 1 South, and follow signs to Boston.

IN THE AREA

Accommodations

Amelia Payson House, 16 Winter Street, Salem. Phone: 978-744-8304; www.ameliapaysonhouse.com. A bed & breakfast inn serving a continental breakfast. Open Apr.–Oct. Inexpensive to expensive.

Crowne Plaza Boston North Shore, 50 Ferncroft Road, Danvers. Phone: 978-777-2500; http://cpbostonns.com. Inexpensive to moderate.

Emerson Inn-by-the-Sea, Rockport. Phone: 800-964-5550; www.emersoninnbythesea.com. Range of rooms from inexpensive to expensive.

Hawthorne Hotel, 18 Washington Square, Salem. Phone: 978-744-4080; www.hawthornehotel.com. Inexpensive to moderate.

Dining

Clam Box, 246 High Street, Ipswich. Phone: 978-356-9707; www.ipswich ma.com/clambox. Fried clams, of course, plus other seafood and burgers. Inexpensive to moderate. Call for open hours.

Danversport Yacht Club, 161 Elliott Street, Danvers. Phone: 978-774-8620; www.danversport.com. Grille and Bistro open daily except Mon. for lunch and dinner. Moderate.

Elliott's at the Blackburn, 2 Main Street, Gloucester. Phone: 978-282-1919; www.elliottsattheblackburn.com. Open Tues.–Sat., 4–close; Sun. brunch 11–close. Inexpensive (pizza) to moderate.

Nathaniel's at the Hawthorne Hotel, 18 Washington Square, Salem. Phone: 978-825-4311; www.hawthornehotel.com/dining. Elegant dining. Moderate to expensive.

Red's Sandwich Shop, 15 Central Street, Salem. Phone: 978-745-3527; www.redssandwichshop.com. Open daily for breakfast and lunch. Inexpensive.

Sam & Joe's Café, 30 Water Street, Danvers. Phone: 978-774-6262; www.samandjoescafe.com. A local landmark since 1956, known throughout the North Shore for its thin-crust pizza and other Italian specialities. Open daily for lunch and dinner. Inexpensive.

The Tavern at the Hawthorne Hotel, 18 Washington Square, Salem. Phone: 978-825-4342; www.hawthornehotel.com/dining. A friendly bar and informal restaurant. Inexpensive.

Woodman's, Route 133, Essex. Phone: 978-768-6057; www.woodmans .com. All kinds of fried seafood plus lobsters, lobster rolls, and chowders. Open daily for lunch and dinner. Moderate.

Attractions and Recreation

Cape Ann Light Station, Thacher Island, Rockport. Phone; 978-546-7697; www.thacherisland.org. A small launch ferries passengers to Thacher Island on Wed. at 9 and on Sat. at 9 and 10, weather permitting. Advance reservations are required. Climb the tower, explore the island, and visit the keeper's house. Call for details and launch site. $30. If you happen to have a kayak with you or want to rent one in town, you can kayak out on your own.

Castle Hill and Crane Beach, Ipswich. Open dawn to dusk throughout the year. Information: www.thetrustees.org/places-to-visit/northeast-ma /castle-hill-on-the-crane.html. Fee charged.

Derby House, Derby Street, Salem. Phone: 978-740-1650; www.nps.gov /sama/historyculture/derby.htm. The Derby House is part of the National Park Service Salem Maritime National Historic Site. The Park Service offers tours of the historic Georgian-style home overlooking the harbor. See website for details of tours of this and other park properties. Small fee.

Derby Wharf Light Station, Derby Wharf, Salem. Contact: www.nps .gov/sama/historyculture/lighthouse.htm. The lighthouse has been in place here since 1871. Although you can't enter the lighthouse, the half-mile walk out to it as a breeze blows along historic Derby Wharf is a good excursion on a hot summer day.

Essex Shipbuilding Museum, 66 Main Street, Essex. Phone: 978-768-7541; www.essexshipbuildingmuseum.com. Open June–Oct., Wed.–Sun., 10–5; Nov.–May, Sat.–Sun., 10–5. Closed Jan. 1–Mar. 14 except for groups. Small fee charged.

The Clam Box Restaurant in Ipswich is a North Shore landmark.

Friendship, Derby Wharf, Salem. Contact: www.nps.gov/sama/history culture/Friendshiphistory.htm. Owned by the National Park Service, tours of the ship give an informative peek at Salem's long-ago maritime dominance. Small fee.

Glen Magna, Ingersoll Street, Danvers. Phone: 978-777-1666; www .danvershistory.org/buildings/glen.html. Grounds are open weekdays 9–dusk and Sat.–Sun., 9–noon unless an event is taking place on the property. Donation, $2. House tours, including a box lunch, May–Oct. by reservation; $20.

House of the Seven Gables, 115 Derby Street, Salem. Phone: 978-744-0991; www.7gables.org. Open July 1–Oct. 31, 10–7; Nov. 1–Dec. 30, 10–5; closed Jan. 1–14. Adults, $12.50; seniors, $11.50; children 5–12, $7.50. Admission includes a guided tour and entrance to other buildings on the site and to the gardens.

National Park Service Regional Visitor Center, Essex Street, Salem. Phone: 978-740-1650; www.nps.gov/sama. Open year-round. Offers inexpensive tours.

National Park Service Salem Maritime Historic Site, Derby Street, Salem. Phone: 978-740-1650; www.nps.gov/sama.

Peabody Essex Museum, 161 Essex Street. Phone: 978-745-9500; www.pem.org. Open Tues.–Sun., 10–5 and some Mon. holidays. Adults, $15; seniors, $13; students, $11; ages 16 and under, free. Admission to Yin Yu Tang House, additional $5.

Putnam House, 431 Maple Street, Danvers. Phone: 978-777-1666 (Danvers Historical Society); www.danvershistory.org/buildings/putnam.html. Open by appointment.

Rebecca Nurse Homestead, 149 Pine Street, Danvers. Phone: 978-774-8799; www.rebeccanurse.org. A replica of the 1672 Village Meeting House can also be visited. There is a monument to Rebecca Nurse, whose family buried her in an unmarked grave, in the Nurse family cemetery on the west side of the property. Open June 15 through Labor Day, Fri.–Sun., 10–4; Sept. through Oct., Sat.–Sun., 9–4. Other times by appointment. Adults, $6.50; seniors, $5; children, $4.50.

Rocky Neck Art Colony, 53 Rocky Neck Avenue, Gloucester. Contact: www.rockyneckartcolony.org. Largely seasonal, but some artists' galleries may be open in the off-season. See website for details.

Salem Witch Museum, Washington Square, Salem. Phone: 978-744-1692; www.salemwitchmuseum.com. Open 10–5 daily and 10–7 in July and Aug. Extended hours during the fall Haunted Happenings celebration that celebrates Halloween throughout much of Oct. Adults, $8.50; seniors, $7; children 6–14, $5.50.

Schooner *Thomas E. Lannon,* Seven Seas Wharf at the Gloucester House Restaurant, Rogers Street (Route 127), Gloucester. Phone: 978-281-6634; www.schooner.org. Seasonal trips include lobster cruises and sunset sails. Phone or see website for details.

7 Seas Whale Watch, 63 Rogers Street (Route 127), Gloucester. Phone: 1-888-283-1776; www.7seas-whalewatch.com. Departures vary with the season; call or check website. Adults: $45; seniors, $39; under 16, $29; ages 3 and under, free.

Singing Beach, Beach Street, Manchester-by-the-Sea. Contact: www
.manchester.ma.us/Pages/ManchesterMA_Recreation/singingbeach. Parking fee charged in season. See website for nonresident parking regulations
and parking options.

Stage Fort Park, Hough Street, Gloucester. Phone: 978-281-8865;
www.seecapeann.com. Open all year; parking fee in season.

Wingaersheek Beach, off Concord and Atlantic Streets, Gloucester.
Phone: 978-281-9785 (Parks Department). Concession stand, restrooms,
showers. Parking, $20 weekdays; $25 weekends.

Witch House, 310½ Essex Street, Salem. Phone: 978-744-8815; salem
web.com/witchhouse. Architecturally interesting, the house is typical of
early New England saltbox style. Open daily May–early Nov., 10–5;
extended hours and special events in Oct. Guided tours: Adults, $10.25;
seniors, $8.25; children 7–14, $6.25. Self-guided tours, deduct $2. Chil-
dren 6 and under, free.

Shopping

Americana Antiques, 48 Main Street, Essex. Phone: 978-768-6006;
www.americanaantiques.com.

Antiques Gallery, 69 Wharf Street, Salem. Phone: 978-741-3113;
www.pickeringwharf.com.

Bearskin Neck Leathers, 7 Old Harbor Road, Bearskin Neck, Rockport.
Phone: 978-546-2258; www.bearskinneckleather.com.

Cat 'n' the Fiddle, 61 Wharf Street, Salem. Phone: 978-741-0060.

Rockport Fudgery, Tuna Wharf, Bearskin Neck, Rockport. Phone: 1-
888-383-4379; www.rockportfudgery.com.

Other Contacts

Cape Ann information: www.seecapeann.com.

North Shore information: www.northofboston.org.

The Hail to the Sunrise *monument in Charlemont*

CHAPTER

5

Massachusetts: The Mohawk Trail

Estimated length: About 80 miles from Boston to Mile 63 at Erving and the start of the Mohawk Trail tour; about 100 miles to drive the Mohawk Trail and side trips.

Estimated time: About two hours from Boston to Erving; a few hours to a day to enjoy the Mohawk Trail.

Getting there: Take Route 2 West from Boston toward Concord. (This is also called the Concord Turnpike.) Follow Route 2 to Erving.

Highlights: Driving the **Mohawk Trail,** you'll be traveling where Native Americans once walked along a narrow path that wound through woods and beside rushing water, all against a backdrop of picturesque rolling hills. Now charmingly kitschy, today's trail combines small-town history, souvenir shops, restaurants that serve the best of American road food, and lovely scenery in one short but memorable drive. Plan to come here from late May through October for ease of travel and when most accommodations and restaurants are open, although a drive along the trail in winter, perhaps combined with skiing in the nearby Berkshires, has its own appeal.

Nearly a hundred years ago, the Commonwealth of Massachusetts designated the **Mohawk Trail** as a scenic tourist route, the first of many accolades to come its way that also include recognition as a National Scenic Byway. A couple of generations ago, a drive along the trail was as much a part of most New England families' vacation plans as theme-park trips are now. Today, there's a certain '40s and '50s nostalgia to the trail. Time may not stand still here, but it seems to move at a slower pace.

The original trail is thought to have been a footpath about 18 inches wide, just sufficient for walking single file. Native Americans from several tribes probably used it to travel between hunting, fishing, and planting sites and to trade with one another. Arrival of the first permanent white settlers changed the once-peaceful dynamic between the Native peoples, who before long were engaged in fighting each other, thus making it easier for the newcomers to take over portions of their tribal lands. Over time, the trail would be widened, first to allow passage of horses and wagons, and eventually to accommodate the automobile travel that would make the Mohawk Trail, now a portion of Route 2, a popular tourist destination.

Starting at its eastern end at Mile 63 in **Erving**, the Mohawk Trail is clearly indicated by signs that have long guided travelers along their way. This is an area of small, rural New England towns, gurgling rivers, and state parks like **Erving State Park,** where you may want to pause for a walk or a bike ride. Trail maps are available online or at the park; an interesting 1-mile loop opens to lovely views of New Hampshire's Mount Monadnock in the distance. Or, you can fish or go for a swim in the park's Laurel Lake, carved out eons ago by a glacier.

A herd of ceramic cows greets your arrival at the **Wagon Wheel Restaurant** in nearby **Gill**, a must stop if you are in the area at mealtime. Commemorative plates decorate the walls, Bakelite clocks tell the time (or not), and plastic radios crank out '50s classics like Dee Clark's "Hey Little Girl." There's even a shelf of traditional board games to keep antsy children happy or just to while away an hour. In the best tradition of American road food, the menu choices and the portions are both substantial, and the food is terrific.

You might not expect to find an emu farm on a New England byway, but sure enough, **Songline Emu Farm** is flourishing on Route 2 in **Gill**. The oil of emus, a bird native to Australia, is made into a variety of cosmetics and lotions said to help an array of skin and joint conditions.

From Gill, turn south onto Main Road through **Turners Falls**. The downtown area, with its historic 19th-century buildings, has a number of artists' galleries and shops. Many people stop in Turners Falls to visit **Our**

Lady of Czestochowa Roman Catholic Church. Named for the famous Black Madonna icon that is one of the national symbols of Poland, the church is often open to the public for viewing of its stained-glass windows and intricately carved wooden altars.

Turners Falls is also home to the **Great Falls Discovery Center**, making good use of several old mill buildings that were once the heart and soul of the town. Dedicated to preserving the natural habitat of the Connecticut River Watershed, the center has walking trails and butterfly gardens, as well as open areas for viewing birds and wildlife, and hosts programs about environmental issues, including many of interest to children.

From Turners Falls, head back to Route 2 West. After about 2 miles, turn onto Route 5 South and drive 6 miles to **Historic Deerfield.** The village of Deerfield has a long and intriguing history, beginning in 1669 when it was a remote British outpost. Decades of ongoing skirmishes between the British and Native Americans ultimately resulted in many tribal members joining forces with French Canadians, who also had an interest in the area. On February 29, 1704, a French and Indian raid resulted in the deaths of 56 Deerfield residents, the capture of many others, and the almost total destruction of the village.

TRAIL TRAVELERS

Many famous people have traveled the Mohawk Trail, including Benedict Arnold, who in 1775 led an expedition through the area while en route to Fort Ticonderoga in New York State. Still devoted to the American cause at the time, he persuaded additional troops to join him along the way and successfully captured British armaments at the fort, returning via the trail to carry the spoils back to Boston. New England writers said to have been inspired by the trail's rugged beauty include Henry David Thoreau, Ralph Waldo Emerson, and Nathaniel Hawthorne.

Eventually Deerfield was reestablished, and today a highlight of a visit to this area is a stop at the part of town designated as Historic Deerfield, a fascinating mile-long stretch of homes and a tavern dating from the 18th and 19th centuries, most of them still on their original sites. The homes are a microcosm of early New England life, showing how buildings changed to meet the needs of the families that occupied them.

The Sheldon House, for example, was built between 1754 and 1757 for a family of farmers; by 1802 an ell had been added to accommodate the three generations then living on the property. The Barnard Tavern, built in 1795, would have been at the heart of village life. It was here that residents

The 1734 Allen House at Historic Deerfield

got news of the wider world from stagecoach drivers and their passengers, who stopped for a meal or an overnight stay before continuing their journeys. The tavern also served as a kind of community center where dances, celebrations, and meetings were held. Even if your travels bring you to Deerfield when the buildings are closed, it's worth pulling over to walk along the street and envision what life was like here more than 200 years ago.

Candles played an important role in the life of the colonists, so perhaps it's fitting that **Yankee Candle Co.,** manufacturer of the popular line of scented candles, is based in nearby South Deerfield, about 5 miles south of Historic Deerfield on Route 5. At this self-proclaimed "Scenter of the Universe," there's plenty to interest the whole family, from learning about the manufacturing process to trying your hand at creating your own candle.

To return to Route 2 and the Mohawk Trail, head north on Route 5, driving through **Greenfield**, the county seat. Head west toward **Shelburne Falls.** Depending on the season, you may see farmers at work in their fields, gardeners tending their flower beds, maple-syrup producers tapping their trees or sugaring off—the process of boiling maple sap into maple syrup— or those same maple trees blazing with fall color. Try to time things so that you'll pass the **Mohawk Diner** in time for breakfast or lunch. Tucked away in a strip mall, the diner looks unprepossessing from the outside; within, it's an entirely different story because here you'll be served traditional diner food with a gourmet twist (think homemade sauces and shitake mushrooms, for example).

About a mile down the road is the **Mohawk Trading Post,** one of the few remaining businesses on the Mohawk Trail offering Native American–made articles. There is a nice assortment of sterling silver jewelry and beadwork made by Native peoples of the United States and Canada, as well as the usual souvenirs made elsewhere.

Be sure to bring your camera when you stop in downtown **Shelburne Falls.** To get there, turn left off Route 2 onto South Maple Street and take the first left onto Bridge Street. You may never complain about potholes in the road again after visiting the falls that give this village its name, and you'll definitely want some photographic proof of what you're seeing. Beginning when the last glaciers melted, the potholes beneath the falls were carved out by rushing water carrying heavy loads of sand and stones that eventually eroded the base of the Deerfield River. The potholes' size ranges from 6 inches to a whopping 39 feet. The erosion process continues when the river swells with each spring's runoff.

Shelburne Falls' photogenic **Bridge of Flowers** is an old trolley bridge across the river that a gardener and community volunteers keep massed with 500 varieties of flowers and shrubs, from early spring to first frost. To see the last of the trolleys that once used the bridge, stop in at the nearby **Shelburne Falls Trolley Museum,** where you can ride the trolley, pump a handcar, and indulge your inner conductor by playing with model trains.

You may want to end your visit to Shelburne Falls with a little shopping. Many artists and craftspeople have moved into town in recent years, lining the streets with funky little stores and galleries that have helped revitalize the community. The **Ann Brauer Quilt Studio** sells intricate, abstract quilts far different from traditional country patterns. You can observe glassblowing at **Young & Constantin Gallery** or visit a pottery studio overlooking the Bridge of Flowers at **Bald Mountain Pottery Studio & Gallery.**

From Shelburne Falls, the Mohawk Trail winds on toward the rural community of **Charlemont**. Between the two communities, you'll pass the

Big Indian Shop, long a local landmark. Inside, you'll find everything from lovely native crafts to kitschy souvenirs. To visit a covered bridge, turn onto Route 8A North; the **Bissell Bridge** is just a few hundred feet away. Park in the nearby parking lot, because the bridge is open to foot traffic only.

There may be other places where you can simultaneously shower and gaze out the window at chickens and roosters pecking for their breakfast, but none is likely to be as charming as the **Warfield House Inn**. Located on a short, winding road that juts abruptly to the north off Route 2, the inn is a working farm that's also home to ducks, llamas, horses, sheep, goats, cows, and friendly dogs and cats. Deer roam the meadows. In spring you can watch maple syrup being made; in winter, snowshoes are piled on the front porch, an invitation to explore the inn's 530 acres. If you want to get away from it all, this is the place.

Atop an enormous boulder beside Route 2, just a few minutes past the

The Shelburne Falls carve out enormous potholes in the riverbed below.

inn on the left, a 900-pound bronze casting of a Native American looks across the Deerfield River, a permanent memorial to the tribes who walked the original Mohawk Trail. Titled *Hail to the Sunrise,* the statue of a rugged brave faces east, arms upraised to the Great Spirit. A small park surrounding the statue contains 100 stones inscribed with the names of tribes from across the United States.

Almost across the street, the **Mohawk Park Restaurant** is a convenient stopping point. The specials offered a few nights a week bring out local families, making this a comfortable place if you're traveling with children. You'll need to eat heartily to be ready for all the outdoor activity available in Charlemont, most of it centered around the Deerfield River, where you can go whitewater rafting or kayaking with companies like **Crabapple Whitewater, Inc.** or **Moxie,** to get a real feel for the river that has played such an important role in the history of this region. One wonders what the local Native Americans would have thought to see

Stop at the Big Indian Shop for a Mohawk Trail souvenir.

human beings in helmets and harnesses suspended from cables arcing through the trees, but if you've ever wanted to experience a zip line, here's your chance. In addition to water-based activities, **Zoar** offers zip line tours of the forest canopy, an unforgettable way to explore the area.

If you'd like a quieter exploration of the local woods, visit the **Mohawk Trail State Forest,** a portion of which runs beside Route 2. Find your own spot among its more than 6,000 acres to enjoy a picnic or a swim, or inquire about hiking a portion of the original Mohawk Trail that is still a foot trail through the forest.

This historical marker along the trail tells the tale of thrifty Yankees.

Leaving Charlemont and heading through Savoy and other small towns into Florida (yes, Florida, Massachusetts!), you'll drive along one of the prettiest and most pristine parts of the Mohawk Trail. Here the road twists and turns through the foothills of the Berkshire Mountains. At Whitcomb Summit, you will have reached the highest point on the trail, at 2,173 feet. To enjoy the panoramic view at its fullest, consider staying overnight at the **Whitcomb Summit Motel**.

Descending into North Adams via the Mohawk Trail's famous Hairpin Curve, you'll pass the **Golden Eagle Restaurant and Lounge**, another restaurant with spectacular views. From there, continue on into **North Adams.** Once known for textiles and shoe manufacturing, North Adams has undergone a resurgence thanks to the downtown presence of the Massachusetts Museum of Contemporary Art, popularly known as **MASS MoCA.**

Housed in a former factory complex of 26 buildings, MASS MoCA presents films and a variety of performing arts in addition to contemporary sculpture and other art in indoor and outdoor exhibition spaces.

In **Williamstown,** you've reached the end of the Mohawk Trail. Home to Williams College, Williamstown is a typical New England college town whose buildings still reflect its colonial roots. If you're not saturated with art after a MoCA visit, stop in at the **Williams College Museum of Art,** with its impressive array of paintings and sculpture and the largest collection anywhere of works by artists Maurice and Charles Prendergast. There's interesting shopping in town, including at **Where'd You Get That?,** a store that offers gifts "for the curious," where you'll find a wide array of games, puzzles, puppets, and other fun stuff.

Williamstown is a bustling community centered around the college, so at almost any time of year you'll find a concert, theatrical production, or festival taking place in town. **The Williams Inn** has a long tradition of accommodating both Williams college parents and visitors along the Mohawk Trail for overnight stays or meals in its excellent restaurant and tavern.

Return to Boston on Route 2 or, for an alternative drive, head south on Route 7 toward Pittsfield. Just beyond Pittsfield, bear left on Route 20 to the Massachusetts Turnpike (I-90) and head east to Boston.

THE ELK AT THE TOP OF THE TRAIL

The impressive sculpture of an elk that greets travelers near the summit of the Mohawk Trail was erected in 1923 as a memorial to members of the Order of the Elks who died in World War I.

REMEMBERING SUSAN B. ANTHONY

Feminist, suffragette, and abolitionist, Susan B. Anthony was born in 1820 in Adams, Massachusetts, where she spent the first six years of her life. Born into a Quaker family, in adulthood she made her reputation as a tireless social reformer, especially in the cause of women, who in mid-19th-century New England had virtually no political influence. With Elizabeth Cady Stanton she was cofounder of the National Women's Suffrage Association, and together they began the long battle to win the right to vote for women. Anthony's Adams birthplace sat empty for several years before being recently restored and opened to the public. To visit her home at 67 East Road in Adams, take Route 8 south from North Adams. After about 4 miles, turn left onto Lime Street, then right onto East Road for about 1.5 miles.

IN THE AREA

Accommodations

Deerfield Inn, 81 Main Street, Deerfield. Phone: 1-800-926-3865; www
.deerfieldinn.com. Built in 1884, this attractive inn has long been a popular stop. Moderate.

The Williams Inn, Route 2 (on the Williams College campus), Williamstown. Phone: 800-828-0133; www.williamsinn.com. A large inn with a restaurant and informal tavern, both serving meals. Noted for Sunday brunch. Moderate to expensive.

Warfield House Inn, 200 Warfield Road, Charlemont. Phone: 1-888-339-8439; www.warfieldhouseinn.com. A bed & breakfast inn and working farm serving a country breakfast to guests. Inexpensive.

Whitcomb Summit Motel, Mohawk Trail (Route 2), Florida. Phone: 413-662-2625; www.whitcombsummit.com. Rooms, individual cabins, hiking and biking trails, excellent views, and a convenient café. Inexpensive to moderate.

Dining

Champney's at the Deerfield Inn, 81 Main Street, Deerfield. Phone: 413-774-5587; www.champneysrestaurant.com. Serves dinner Fri.–Mon. Tavern open seven nights a week with a light menu. Dining room: Moderate. Tavern: Inexpensive.

Golden Eagle Restaurant and Lounge, Mohawk Trail (Route 2), Clarksburg, on the historic Hairpin Curve. Phone: 413-663-9834; www.thegoldeneaglerestaurant.com. Fine-dining restaurant and informal lounge. Open for lunch and dinner. Inexpensive to moderate.

Mohawk Diner, Mohawk Trail (Route 2), Shelburne Falls. Phone: 413-625-6643. Open daily for breakast and lunch. Inexpensive.

Mohawk Park Restaurant, Mohawk Trail (Route 2), Charlemont. Phone: 413-339-4470. Inexpensive.

Hairpin Curve on the Mohawk Trail

Wagon Wheel Restaurant, 39 French King Highway (Route 2), Gill.
Phone: 413-863-8210. Worth a stop, even if it's just to grab a coffee or a
locally made Harmony Springs soda and be transported back to a simpler
time. Open early to 8 PM. Inexpensive.

Attractions and Recreation

Crabapple Whitewater, Inc., Mohawk Trail (Route 2), Charlemont.
Phone: 1-800-5553-7238; www.crabappleinc.com. Easy to advanced
whitewater-rafting trips, some suitable for ages five and up, as well as
inflatable kayak trips. Call for details on trips and prices.

Erving State Park, Mohawk Trail (Route 2), Erving. Phone: 978-544-
3939; www.mass.gov/dcr/parks/central/ervf.htm. Eight miles of roads
loop through this scenic park, a great place to stop with a picnic lunch.

Great Falls Discovery Center, 2 Avenue A, Turners Falls. Phone: 413-863-3221; www.greatfallsma.org. Summer hours, daily 10–4; in winter open Fri.–Sat. 10–4. Free; some programs may have small fees.

Historic Deerfield, Deerfield. Phone: 413-775-7214; www.historic -deerfield.org. Open Apr.–Dec. except major holidays, 9:30–4:30. Call for winter hours. Stop at the Hall Tavern Visitor Center for tour information.

MASS MoCA, 87 Marshall Street, North Adams. Phone: 413-MoCA111; www.massmoca.org. Contemporary art exhibits, films, performances. Special art activities for children on weekends. Check website for the latest happenings. From Sept.–late June, open daily 11–5 except closed Tues. From late June through early Sept., open daily 11–6. Adults, $15; students, $10; ages 6–16, $5; under five, free.

Mohawk Trail State Forest, Mohawk Trail (Route 2), Charlemont. Phone: 413-339-5504; www.mass.gov/dcr/parks/western/mhwk.htm. Open year-round.

Moxie, 1 Thunder Road, Charlemont. Phone: 1-800-866-9643; www .moxierafting.com. Rafting and kayaking trips for ages five and up at a variety of skill levels. Call for details on trips and prices.

Our Lady of Czestochowa Roman Catholic Church, 84 K Street, Turners Falls. Contact: http://chroniclesofczestochowa.org. The church, which retains many of the Polish traditions of settlers in the area, is known as the Gem of Franklin County.

Shelburne Falls Trolley Museum, 14 Depot Street, Shelburne Falls. Phone: 413-625-9443; www.sftm.org. Open May through Oct., Sat., Sun., and holidays, 11–5. In July and Aug., also open on Mon. 1–5. Adults, $3; children $1.50; ages 5 and under free. Fee includes trolley rides.

Susan B. Anthony Birthplace, 67 East Road, Adams. Phone: 413-743-7121; www.susanbanthonybirthplace.com. Call or check website for open hours.

Williams College Museum of Art, Route 2, Williamstown. Phone: 413-597-2429; www.wcma.org. Free admission.

Zoar, 7 Main Street, Charlemont. Phone: 1-800-532-7483; www.zoar outdoor.com. Rafting, kayaking, biking, rock climbing adventures, and zip lines. On-site lodging. Call for details on trips and prices.

Shopping

Ann Brauer Quilt Studio, 2 Conway Street, Shelburne Falls. Phone: 413-625-8605; www.annbrauer.com. Call for open hours.

Bald Mountain Pottery Studio & Gallery, 28 State Street, Shelburne Falls. Phone: 413-625-8110; www.baldmountainpottery.blogspot.com. Open year-round; call for open hours.

Big Indian Shop, Mohawk Trail (Route 2), between Shelburne Falls and Charlemont. Phone: 413-625-6817. Call for open hours.

Mohawk Trading Post, Mohawk Trail (Route 2), Shelburne Falls. Phone: 413-625-2412; www.mohawk-trading-post.com. Open all year; call for winter hours.

Songline Emu Farm, 66 French King Highway (Route 2), Gill. Phone: 413-863-2700; www.songlineemufarm.com. A wide variety of skincare products available in the farm store. Open Thurs.–Sat., 12–5.

Where'd You Get That? 100 Spring Street, Williamstown. Phone: 413-458-2206; www.wygt.com. Open daily 10–6, except Sun. 10–5.

Yankee Candle Company, 25 Greenfield Road, South Deerfield. Phone: 877-636-7707; www.yankeecandle.com. Thousands of candles, a Bavarian Village, a Nutcracker exhibit, and lots of hands-on exhibits and events welcome visitors to the popular flagship store. Open daily 10–6 except Thanksgiving and Christmas.

Young & Constantin Gallery, 4 Deerfield Avenue, Shelburne Falls. Phone: 1-866-625-6422; www.yandcglass.com.

Other Contacts

Mohawk Trail information: www.mohawktrail.com.

A statue in Alton honors Civil War soldiers.

CHAPTER

6

New Hampshire: The Lakes Region

Estimated length: About 40 miles from Manchester to Alton; about 100 miles to tour the region.

Estimated time: About one hour from Manchester. The tour itself can be a pleasant afternoon drive or an overnight stay to enjoy more of the area's attractions.

Getting there: From Manchester take Route 28 north to Alton.

Highlights: There are nearly three hundred lakes and ponds in the New Hampshire Lakes Region; this tour includes **Big and Little Squam Lakes** as well as **Lake Winnipesaukee.** The route combines stretches of bucolic country driving with the summertime hustle-bustle to be expected around **Wolfeboro** on Lake Winnipesaukee, the oldest summer resort in the country, and the lively, kitschy atmosphere of the area around **Weirs Beach.** Beautiful lakeside vistas and mountain views, scenic boat trips, hiking, crafts made by New Hampshire artisans, antiquing, and excellent dining and attractive accommodations are part of the appeal of the Lakes Region. Try to visit from late spring through mid-October, when the scenery is at its best and most attractions are open.

On this tour, you'll first pass through **Alton** on Route 11, a small town on the southern end of Lake Winnipesaukee with a tiny, picturesque village green or "common." Alton was once a regular stop for steamships, and you can still take a leisurely cruise on Lake Winnipesaukee aboard the *Mount Washington,* which has plied the water here since 1872. A more unusual option is a ride aboard the oldest floating post office in the United States. The mailboat *Sophie C.* brings passengers along for the ride as it delivers mail to several inhabited islands. Aboard the mailboat you can mail post-cards with a special stamp, a neat little gift for collectors. These boats and others are run by **Mount Washington Cruises**. One of the *Mount Washington*'s stops is in the part of Alton known as **Alton Bay,** near the former train station. If you'd rather watch boats come and go instead of getting on one, walk around to the back of the train station, where a bench offers a secluded spot to sit and look out over the water.

NEW HAMPSHIRE'S FAVORITE FISHING SPOT

Called Lake Winni by locals, Lake Winnipesaukee's name comes from a Native American phrase meaning "smile of the Great Spirit." The largest lake in New Hampshire and the sixth-largest naturally formed lake in the country, Lake Winnipesaukee is known by anglers the world over for its wonderful bass fishing. Three mountain ranges—the White Mountains, Belknap Range, and the Ossipee Range—provide a dramatic backdrop in any season, but never more beautifully than in the fall.

Leaving Alton Bay, drive west on Route 11 toward Laconia. Along the way you'll be treated to scenic views of the lake and the mountains that ring it. You'll find several pull-offs designed to accommodate photographers. There are also multiple hiking trails in this area, so if—only if—you've come fully equipped to hike in New England's changeable weather and always rocky terrain, you may want to spend some time hiking here. One popular option is **Mount Major Trail**. The parking lot will be on your left about 4 miles after you leave Alton Bay. This is a loop trail of about 3.4 miles, which most people complete in about three hours. Moderately difficult overall, it has some very rugged patches here and there, all rewarded by expansive views from the top.

If hiking's not your thing, you can still enjoy being outside, at **Ellacoya State Park**. You'll find it in Gilford, about 10 miles north of Alton Bay; bear right following signs to the park. You might want to pick up a picnic lunch to eat while enjoying the 600-foot-long sandy beach and views of the mountains. Ellacoya is just one of several state parks sprinkled around the lake.

Back on Route 11 in Gilford, check out the **Fireside Inn** if you're plan-

Lake Winnipesaukee ringed by mountains

ning to spend a night or two in the area. **Patrick's Pub & Eatery**, right across the street, makes this a convenient stop.

At the traffic light in Gilford, turn right onto Route 11-B and follow the signs to **Weirs Beach** if you're up for what some consider down-home fun (others find it a little too honky-tonk for their taste). There's a public beach and a boardwalk, along with plenty of fast-food joints, nightclubs, arcades, souvenir shops, go-kart tracks, and dozens of other attractions, including music events and fireworks. During the annual mid-June Motorcycle Week in nearby Laconia, things get especially colorful (bikini bike wash, anyone?) when some thirty thousand bikers arrive for the largest motorcycle rally in the country.

If you'd rather bypass the crowds at Weirs, or come back later in the day, at the Gilford traffic light turn left onto Route 3 and head south to **Laconia** past scenic Paugus Bay. Turning right at the intersection of Routes 3 and 107 will bring you through a miracle mile of fast-food restaurants and stores. Hang in there, because eventually your tour will continue on roads less traveled. Turn right at the stoplight onto Route 106 North, which will bring you into the center of Laconia, a good stopping-off point if you need to shop for some forgotten item. Otherwise, continue to the traffic circle and head north on Route 3 into **Meredith**.

After about 0.5 mile, on the right, you'll come to a retail gallery of the **League of New Hampshire Craftsmen**. If you're interested in quality crafts, you'll want to stop here. Everything in the shop—and in the league's six other retail galleries across the state—has met rigorous standards. You'll find a wide range to choose from that includes everything from metal items to weaving.

Each year in late July, Meredith hosts an **Antique and Classic Boat Show** that brings more than 80 beautifully restored Chris-Craft, Century, Gar Wood, and other vintage boats to the town docks. Some are trucked in, but many come under their own power, and it's a treat to watch them arrive. The proud owners are always happy to talk about them. Various judging events take place during the day while the boats remain on display.

From Meredith, continue on Route 3 into **Holderness**, where you'll find **Big Squam** and **Little Squam Lakes**. Movie buffs may find the town strangely familiar. Hollywood made it famous when *On Golden Pond* was filmed here. **Experience Squam Private Boat Excursions & Tours** offers trips that will bring you past many of the most memorable sites in the movie, every bit as beautiful today as they were during the 1981 filming.

If you'd rather stay on dry land, you can get a wonderful meal and a lovely view of Little Squam Lake from **Walter's Basin Restaurant & Pub**. Wide windows open onto the lake, and you can dine inside, outside, or in the cheerful pub. Just beyond the restaurant, the **Holderness General Store** sells old-fashioned penny candy and plenty of it (of course, the penny candy now starts at about 15 cents apiece), wheels of cheese, gelato, fat deli sandwiches, fudge, trail maps, bug repellent, and in the true spirit of country stores, just about anything else you might want. Across the street, you can use the local library's wi-fi to check e-mail.

Leaving the center of Holderness, turn right onto Route 113 to the **Squam Lakes Natural Science Center**. In this fascinating place you can wander along trails that wind through forested areas and across marshes and meadows, getting up close and personal with native animals housed in woodland enclosures. Expect to see, among many other creatures, black bears, mountain lions, bobcats, and a variety of raptors. You can also tour

Big Squam Lake on the Science Center's pontoon boat or visit lovely gardens on the site. Allow a few hours if you plan to do it all. This is a fun stop for all ages and a must for traveling families.

Back on Route 113, you'll quickly come across other hiking options on both sides of the road, including Cotton Mountain Trail and Mount Morgan Trail on the left, and a local favorite, West Rattlesnake Trail on the right. Any of these can provide hours of hiking challenges if you've planned ahead and brought hiking gear and supplies.

The road from Holderness to **Sandwich** is one of the prettiest stretches along Route 113. You'll pass old cemeteries and countless stone walls, open fields, and woods—the essence of rural New Hampshire. When you reach the blinking light in the center of Sandwich, turn right and continue about 8 miles to Center Harbor, a pleasant ride beside the lake. Once in Center Harbor, turn left on Route 25, toward **Moultonborough**. If, how-

Picturesque Big Squam Lake in Holderness

ever, you'd first like to take a break and stay overnight, the **Center Harbor Inn** has a pretty lakeside location.

In Moultonborough don't miss the **Old Country Store and Museum**. Built in 1781, it's one of the oldest stores in the country and once accommodated the village post office as well. The second-floor museum is a hodge-podge of "stuff" ranging from tools to the original post office boxes. The store itself sells candy, candles, cookware, clothes—you name it, chances are it's here and you'll have fun poking through everything to find it.

If you've been fortunate enough to hear the haunting tremolo of loons calling from a New Hampshire lake, you can learn more about them at the **Loon Center and Markus Wildlife Sanctuary**. To get there from Route 25, turn right onto Blake Road at the Moultonborough Central School, and at the end of the road, turn right onto Lee's Mill Road. The Loon Center and Sanctuary are on the left. In this beautiful spot stretching along 5,000 feet of shoreline on Lake Winnipesaukee, you can learn everything about loons, from their mating habits, to a typical day in their lives, to the meaning of those otherworldly cries. If you're eager by now to take a break from driving and enjoy a leisurely walk, this is a place to do exactly that. Two pleasant strolls—the 0.25-mile Forest Walk and the 1.5-mile Loon Nest Trail—wind through the sanctuary, taking you through forests and marshes and past brooks and wildflowers. Along the way, you're sure to catch glimpses of loons and other wildlife.

WASTE NOTHING, NOT EVEN ROCKS

Stone walls throughout New Hampshire and the rest of New England have long captured the attention of photographers and poets. Artfully made or hastily heaved together, stone walls are a reminder of the area's agrarian past and the thrifty Yankee tradition of not letting anything go to waste. As early farmers cleared their land for crops and cattle, they uncovered rocks of all sizes that had to be moved out of the way. Soon they were piling them into stone fences to enclose cattle or mark property lines between farms. Stone walls are usually low—perhaps 2 to 3 feet—because hefting the largest stones any higher would have been more than most people could manage alone. It has been estimated that by the mid-1850s there were at least 240,000 stone walls in New England. Some have tumbled down, others have been moved, but many still remain, a picturesque souvenir of a time long gone by. And local gardeners still say—only partly in jest—that the easiest crop to grow in New England is rocks.

The Old Country Store and Museum in Moultonborough

When you leave the sanctuary, return to Route 25, turn right onto Route 109, bear left on Route 171, and travel about 2 miles to visit **Castle in the Clouds**. Back in 1914, an inventor and shoe designer named Tom Pratt built himself a quiet Moultonborough retreat in the form of a 16-room mansion he called Lucknow. Views from the grounds are, in a word, spectacular. The arts and crafts–style home now known as Castle in the Clouds is surrounded by 4,200 acres of forest. You can visit the mansion and walk along 45 miles of trails that wind through the property. The **Carriage House Café** on the premises serves excellent light fare. Many events are held on the grounds including a popular antique and classic car show in July.

Leaving the estate, return to Route 171 and turn left on Route 109 toward Wolfeboro (you'll also see it spelled Wolfeborough) about 15 miles away. The best known of the lakeside towns and the oldest summer resort in the country, Wolfeboro is a good place to base yourself if you'd like to stay in the area for a day or two. The **Wolfeboro Inn** is especially nice in summer, when you can enjoy the private beach or an excursion on the inn's 65-foot *Winnipesaukee Belle*. There's also convenient dining here at **Wolfe's Tavern and Restaurant**.

Once a farming community, Wolfeboro became known as an attractive place to visit when a stagecoach route connecting Dover and Conway wound through town, bringing with it travelers who spread the word about the beauty of this part of New Hampshire. Toward the middle of the 19th century the first hotels were built in Wolfeboro, and visitors began arriving on the *Mount Washington.* By the latter half of the century, tourism was firmly established as a major industry that continues to this day.

No stagecoaches ply their way through modern-day Wolfeboro, but you can hop a trolley at various points for a tour of the town. If you'd rather see Wolfeboro from the water, **Wolfeboro Trolley Tours** also runs boat trips aboard the *Millie B.*

A boat trip like this is a good way to get a feel for the area, since so much of the activity in Wolfeboro centers around Lake Winnipesaukee. The lake has long had a special place in the hearts of vintage boat enthusiasts, so if names like Chris-Craft, Lyman, or Old Town make your own heart flutter, plan a stop at the **New Hampshire Boat Museum** on Route 28/109, about 2 miles north of the village. The history of boating, not just on Lake Winnipesaukee but on other waterways within New Hampshire as well, is chronicled here with displays of outboards, speedboats, sailboats, canoes, and just about everything else related to the boating hobby. If fishing is more your speed, **Angling Adventures** can set you up for fly-fishing and light-tackle angling for bass, trout, salmon, and perch in the company of an experienced guide.

The **Wright Museum** just north of downtown Wolfeboro on Route 28/109 is dedicated entirely to the "Greatest Generation"—those Americans who fought overseas and those who held things down at home dur-

---

LIVE FREE OR DIE

New Hampshire's famous motto, "Live Free or Die," was part of a toast written by the state's most acclaimed military hero, General John Stark. A veteran of both the Battle of Bunker Hill and the Battle of Bennington in Vermont, Stark composed the toast to celebrate the 32nd anniversary of the 1777 Battle of Bennington. Poor health prevented the general from attending the anniversary gathering, but he sent a toast reading, "Live Free or Die: Death is Not the Worst of Evils." His words resonated with those at the celebration and were widely quoted afterward. In 1945 the New Hampshire legislature adopted "Live Free or Die" as the state's official motto.

The Wolfeboro Train Station, now home to the chamber of commerce and an information center

ing World War II. It's a comprehensive look at the years 1939–45, including artifacts such as a 42-ton Pershing tank.

If shopping is still on your agenda, there are a couple of memorable places to visit before you end your lakeside journey. Artisans at **Hampshire Pewter** on Mill Street create a variety of hand-cast decorative and useful items, and factory tours let you see how everything is created. A branch of the **League of New Hampshire Craftsmen** on North Main Street is another chance to find quality handmade creations.

When it's time to wave goodbye to Lake Winni, take Route 28 south to Alton and return to Manchester.

IN THE AREA

Accommodations

Center Harbor Inn, 294 Whittier Highway (Route 25), Center Harbor. Phone: 603-253-4347; www.centerharborinn.com. A wide variety of rooms; rates are room and date specific, ranging from inexpensive to expensive. Check website for details.

Fireside Inn, 17 Harris Shore Road, Gilford. Phone: 1-800-458-3877; www.firesideinngilford.com. Centrally located with a wide range of rooms and suites. Inexpensive to expensive.

Inn at Smith Cove, 19 Roberts Road, Gilford. Phone: 603-293-1111; www.innatsmithcove.com. A lovely Victorian with pretty views of the lake. Inexpensive to moderate.

Wolfeboro Inn, 90 North Main Street, Wolfeboro. Phone: 603-569-3016; www.wolfeboroinn.com. Close to downtown. Moderate to expensive.

Dining

Carriage House Café & Patio, on the grounds of Castle in the Clouds estate, 455 Old Mountain Road, Moultonboro. Phone: 603-476-5900; www.castleintheclouds.org. Open early May through late Oct. for lunch only. Chowders, sandwiches, salads. Inexpensive.

Patrick's Pub & Eatery, Junction of Routes 11 and 11B, Gilford. Phone: 603-293-0841; www.patrickspub.com. A wide variety of soups, salads, and entrées. Open daily for lunch and dinner. Inexpensive to moderate.

Walter's Basin Restaurant & Pub, 859 Route 3, Holderness. Phone: 603-968-4412; www.waltersbasin.com A great spot for fish-and-chips and fish tacos. Pub is popular with locals. Inexpensive to moderate.

Wolfe's Tavern at the Wolfeboro Inn, 90 North Main Street, Wolfboro. Phone: 603-569-3016; www.wolfestavern.com. A friendly and popular local spot for eating and drinking. Open daily for breakfast, lunch, and dinner. Moderate, with inexpensive early-bird specials.

Attractions and Recreation

Angling Adventures, Wolfeboro. Phone: 603-569-6426; www.gadabout golder.com. Fishing trips on Lake Winnipsaukee with an experienced guide. A typical trip lasts four and a half hours; fees include quality rods, reels, lures, flies, and bait, plus snacks, soft drinks, life jackets, and souvenir photos. Usually from late Apr. through mid-Oct. depending on weather. One person, $260; two people, $300; three people, $390. Reservations required. Other trips available.

Antique and Classic Boat Show, Meredith. Contact: www.necacbs.org. Takes place in late July; check website for date and details.

Castle in the Clouds (Lucknow Estate), 455 Old Mountain Road, Moultonborough. Phone: 603-476-5900; www.castleintheclouds.org. Open early May through late Oct. Check website for exact dates. Adults, $15; seniors, $10; children 7–14, $5; ages 6 and under, free. Admission to grounds only, $5; under 7, free.

Ellacoya State Park, Gilford. Phone: 603-293-7821; http://nhstateparks .org. Open all year, but many facilities are open only seasonally; check website for details. Admission: Adults, $4; children 6–11, $2; ages 5 and under, free.

Experience Squam Private Boat Excursions & Tours, Holderness. Phone: 603-968-3990; www.experiencesquam.com. The 21-ft. boat holds 7–9 passengers; lifejackets, coolers, ice, and towels are provided. $215 for two-and-a-half-hour tour; $95 for one hour. Other tours and excursions available.

Loon Center and Markus Wildlife Sanctuary, 183 Lee's Mill Road, Moultonborough. Phone: 603-476-5666; www.loon.org. Open year-round, Mon.–Sat.; also Sun. from July 1 to Columbus Day. Free admission.

Mount Washington Cruises (M/S *Mount Washington* **and M/V** *Sophie C.*)**,** 211 Lakeside Avenue, Weirs Beach, Laconia. Phone: 603-366-5531; www.cruisenh.com. Weirs Beach is the *Mount Washington*'s home port, but you can also board in Wolfeboro, Alton Bay, Center Harbor, or Meredith. Many cruises are offered, ranging from two-and-a-half-hour day cruises to evening dinner cruises. Trips run from late May through late Oct. with additional cruises added during the foliage season, which is quite spectacular at the lake. Day cruises: Adults, $25; children $12; ages 4 and under, free. Sunday jazz and champagne brunch cruise: Adults, $40; children $20; ages 4 and under, free. See website for details on departure times and other cruise options on these boats and two others in the fleet.

New Hampshire Boat Museum, 397 Center Street, Route 28/109, Wolfeboro. Phone: 603-569-4554; www.nhbm.org. Open Memorial Day weekend to Columbus Day weekend, Mon.–Sat., 10–4; Sun. noon–4. Admission: Adults, $5; seniors, $4; students $3, ages 12 and under, free.

Squam Lakes Natural Science Center, 23 Science Center Road, Holderness. Phone: 603-968-7194; www.nhnature.org. Open May 1 through Nov. 1. Adults, $13; seniors, $11; children 3–15, $9; ages 2 and under, free.

Weirs Beach. Information: www.weirsbeach.com. Events and attractions are updated regularly on the website, your best bet for finding out what's happening during the time of your visit.

Wolfeboro Trolley Tours and the *Millie B.,* 60 N. Main Street, Wolfeboro. Phone: 603-569-1080; www.wolfeborotrolley.org. Trolley tours (about 45 minutes) depart daily 10–4 from June 20–Labor Day. Buy tickets from trolley driver or at the Wolfeboro Railroad Station Information Center. Adults, $5; ages 4-12, $3; under age 4, free. From late June to Labor Day, 30-minute tours aboard the *Millie B.* leave daily from 10–4 at the Town Dock. No reservations needed; purchase tickets at the dock. Adults, $20; children 4–12; $10; under 4, free. Lifejackets are provided.

Wright Museum, 77 Center Street, Wolfeboro. Phone: 603-569-1212; www.wrightmuseum.org. Open daily May 1–Oct. 31, 10–4, except on Sun. open noon–4. Closed Nov.–Jan. except for occasional lectures. Open Feb.–Apr., Sun. only, noon–4. Admission: Adults, $8; seniors and veterans, $6; children, $4; under age 4, free.

Shopping

Hampshire Pewter, Mill Street, Wolfeboro. Phone: 1-800-639-7704; www.hampshirepewter.com. Lead-free, handcrafted items ranging from Christmas ornaments to oil lamps, tankards and goblets, and baby gifts. Factory and store open Mon.–Sat., 10–4; factory tours, June 1–Oct. 15.

Holderness General Store, 863 Route 3, Holderness. Phone: 603-968-3446; www.holdernessgeneralstore.net.

League of New Hampshire Craftsmen, 279 Daniel Webster Highway, Meredith. Phone: 603-279-7920. Also at 15 North Main Street, Wolfeboro; phone 603-569-3309. Website for all locations: www.nhcrafts.org. Quality crafts of all kinds here and at the league's other locations.

Old Country Store and Museum, 1011 Whittier Highway, Moultonborough. Phone: 603-476-5750; www.nhcountrystore.com.

Other Contacts

Lakes Region information: www.lakesregion.org.

Area hiking information: www.hike-nh.com.

Sabbaday Falls

CHAPTER

7

New Hampshire: Cruising the Kancamagus Highway

Estimated length: About 93 miles from Manchester to Conway. The Kancamagus Highway is 34.5 miles long.

Estimated time: About 2 hours and 45 minutes from Manchester to Conway. You can drive the Kancamagus in less than an hour, but you won't want to. Depending on your interests, allow time for photographs, a walk or a hike, a swim, or a picnic.

Getting there: From Manchester take I-93 North to Exit 23, Route 104 East. Take Route 3 to Meredith, then Route 25 to Whittier. From Whittier take Route 113 North to Route 16 North and follow it to Conway. Turn left onto Route 112, also known as the Kancamagus Highway.

Highlights: Considered one of the most scenic roads in America, the **Kancamagus Highway,** a designated National Forest Scenic Byway, winds through thick forests and beside scenic rivers, tumbling waterfalls, and rustic swimming holes. To this, add a backdrop of mountains and, in the fall, what many call the most spectacular **fall foliage** in New England, and you begin to understand the appeal of the "Kanc." Yes, this highway has a nickname, perhaps because so few people can wrap their tongues around "Kancamagus." (For the record, it's pronounced Kank-ah-MAW-gus.)

The Kanc is open year-round, weather permitting. Come in the spring for hiking and birdwatching, in the summer for swimming in the Swift River, and in October for that glorious foliage—as long as you're prepared to share the road with lots of other leaf peepers. Assuming the highway hasn't been closed due to heavy snowfalls, winter is also a beautiful time here, and the nearby mountains offer plenty of opportunities for winter sports.

Remember that during this drive you'll be in the heart of the **White Mountain National Forest,** complete with all manner of four-footed residents. Drive carefully and watch for deer, bears, and especially moose, particularly if you drive the Kanc early in the morning or at dusk.

The Kancamagus Highway opened in 1959, providing a route through the White Mountain National Forest between Conway and Lincoln. Beautifully maintained with campgrounds, picnic areas, and clean, if rustic, sanitary facilities, other services are limited. If you'd like to spend a night or two in the area and base yourself at this end of the Kancamagus, your best bet is nearby North Conway, where you can also indulge your inner shopper. The **North Conway Grand Hotel** is in a great location near **Settlers Green Outlet Village,** where tax-free shopping is offered at more than sixty stores. If it's mealtime, try **Horsefeathers** downtown. To get to North Conway from Conway, take Route 16 North. When you're ready to begin your Kancamagus journey, take Route 16 South and turn onto route 112, the Kancamagus Highway.

To do more than simply drive the Kancamagus nonstop, a little advance

---

THE OLD MAN OF THE MOUNTAIN

In his old age he got creaky around the edges and required frequent shoring up just to keep him hanging around. When the end came, sometime during the foggy night of May 2–3, 2003, he was estimated to be somewhere between two thousand and ten thousand years old and had been viewed on his Profile Mountain perch by millions of travelers along I-93, some 65 miles north of Concord. The iconic Old Man of the Mountain, whose 40-ft.-high x 25-ft.-wide face was formed of five ledges of granite (held together in his final years with lots of steel cables and epoxy), is no more, for on that fateful morning early-rising passersby realized that he had finally collapsed. While the state of New Hampshire continues to debate what kind of memorial should be established to its most famous symbol, you can still see his craggy visage on the state quarter, road signs, and souvenirs.

THE FEARLESS ONE

The Kancamagus Highway and several nearby sites bear the names of notable New Hampshire Native Americans. Passaconaway Peak in the White Mountains honors the first Sagamon or great chief of the Penacook Confederacy. Passaconaway united several area tribes into the Penacook Confederacy in 1627, and by all accounts ruled with diplomacy and kept the peace between the tribes and early white settlers for more than forty years. Passaconaway was succeeded first by his son, Wonalancet, and in 1684 by Wonalancet's nephew, Kancamagus, whose name means "the Fearless One." Sadly, Kancamagus would be the last chief of the Penacook Confederacy. Despite his best efforts to maintain the relationships established by his grandfather, bloodshed erupted as white settlers usurped more and more Indian lands. Gruesome battles led to substantial loss of life on both sides. Ultimately the Penacook Confederacy fell apart, and Kancamagus and surviving tribal members retreated to the northern part of the state and, it is assumed, into Canada, where they disappeared from history.

preparation is in order. The most important items may be a full gas tank, plenty of drinking water, and bug repellent from spring through fall. You may want picnic food or snacks, a bathing suit and towel, and old sneakers for wading. Walkers and hikers need appropriate supplies and gear. If you're an inexperienced hiker and unsure what to bring, check with a hiking outfitter or the website hikesafe.com for a list of essential items.

Your drive begins at Conway, where you should stop at the **Saco Ranger Station** just before the start of the Kanc for an inexpensive day pass, necessary if you plan to leave the car at any point. If you just plan to drive through, there's no charge. (Tip: If you forget to buy a pass, there are honor system stands at most pull-offs where you can purchase a day pass and leave the money in an envelope.) Personnel at the Ranger Station will answer questions and supply maps. They also stock a few necessities such as bug spray and hats.

After about 6 miles, turn onto Passaconaway Road to see the photogenic **Albany Covered Bridge**. Built in 1858, the 120-ft. bridge spans the Swift River and is still in regular use. Nearby, old stone walls, cemeteries, and cellar holes are mute reminders of the homesteaders who carved a life out of the wilderness so long ago.

Returning to the Kancamagus, you'll pass numerous scenic pull-offs that make it easy to stop for photos. Many, like the one at **Lower Falls,**

The covered bridge in Albany just off the Kancamagus Highway

have swimming and picnicking areas. On hot summer days, however, the most popular spots for lunch are the large boulders in the middle of the shallow river. Just wade in and choose your rock.

About 2 miles up the road, you'll come to the **Rocky Gorge Scenic Area.** Swimming is not allowed here, but a pleasant, mostly flat, mile-long trail winds around Falls Pond. The beautiful gorge was formed thousands of years ago by a melting glacier.

For a little side trip off the Kanc, just beyond Rocky Gorge turn right onto Bear Notch Road—a scenic drive of about 9 miles with a number of overlooks—into the little town of **Bartlett.** For a pleasant place to stay overnight, turn left onto Route 302 West to the **Bartlett Inn**, about a mile from the light on the left. Bear Notch Road is open May through October, so if you travel here in winter, check the inn's website for alternative routes.

Retracing your route back to the Kancamagus, turn right and watch for signs for the Passaconaway Historic Site, location of the **Russell-Colbath House.** This is the last remaining farmstead in what was once the village of Passaconaway, and one with an intriguing history. Built around 1832, the Cape-style house was built by Thomas Russell and his son, Amzi, and later sold to Amzi, who raised five daughters here with his wife, Eliza. The only daughter to stay in Passaconaway was Ruth, who lived in the house throughout her life. Ruth married a man named Thomas Colbath, and Eliza eventually turned the house over to them. By 1887, the first summer visitors were arriving in the area and needed a post office, which was established in a room in the Russell-Colbath house. Ruth became postmistress, a job she held until 1907.

One day in 1891, Thomas Colbath announced that he was going out "for a while." When he didn't return that evening, his wife lit a lantern in a window for him. It failed to bring Thomas home—for 42 years. Faithful Ruth kept watch for him for 39 of those years before passing away in 1930 at age 80. During those nearly four decades, she maintained the house and property with the assistance of just one local handyman. To everyone's surprise, three years after her death Thomas ambled home, apparently amazed to find his wife dead, the house sold, and the proceeds divided among her relatives. Although no one knows for sure where he went or what he did during the intervening years, it was rumored that he spent them traveling, possibly throughout the world. What *is* known is that, finding a less than warm welcome at his home, he quickly took off once more, never to be heard from again.

The graves of many of the Russell family and Ruth's loyal handyman are in a small cemetery that can be visited on the property. Ruth's grave is angled so she can watch over her home—perhaps still waiting for her wandering husband to return.

OLD THYME GARDENS

On the grounds of the Russell-Colbath House, as at many historic homesteads, gardens give a glimpse into what life was like in a time when people grew not only their own vegetables, but also herbs for medicinal as well as culinary purposes. Thyme for gastric problems, sage, used to soothe sore throats and coughs, mint to aid digestion, and comfrey, made into poultices to apply to bruises, are among the many herbs that grew abundantly in homesteaders' gardens.

Before leaving the Russell-Colbath House, you may want to walk the Rail and River Trail that starts on the property. It's an easy 0.5-mile trail that most people complete within half an hour.

Back on the Kanc, continue on to beautiful **Sabbaday Falls**, a lovely

The Russell-Colbath House

set of falls with swirling pools. For most people it will be an easy walk to the falls from the parking lot. Rubber-soled footwear is a good idea, as there will be some splashing from the falls and there are steps that can be slippery when wet. A few benches are scattered around for rest stops. The name *Sabbaday* comes from Sabbath Day, an old word for Sunday.

Next comes the ear-popping part of your journey when you return to the Kanc and it climbs to its highest point of about 3,000 feet as you approach its terminus at **Lincoln**, passing campgrounds, other trailheads, and scenic overlooks along the way. Just before the highway ends, you'll see **Loon Mountain Resort**, a popular spot with skiers that is now a year-round resort area with plenty of activities to give you a break from driving. If you'd like to stay in the area, try Lincoln's **Red Sleigh Inn** in the home of a former lumber baron, **The Wilderness Inn** in nearby North Woodstock, or the **Bartlett Inn** in Bartlett.

For a real experience in retro kitsch, at the end of the Kanc turn right in Lincoln onto Route 3 to visit **Clark's Trading Post**, a New Hampshire institution since 1928. The original owners began showing black bears as a way of attracting passersby to the trading post, and in 1949 began training them. How you feel about wild animals doing tricks for tourists may be a factor in how much you enjoy the experience here. The trained bears remain a star attraction, but for a single admission price you can also see an acrobatic troupe perform, take a 30-minute train ride through the forest where you'll be greeted by a "wolfman," try your luck on a climbing wall, and wander through various buildings filled with a little of this and a lot of that. There are souvenir shops, of course, and places to get a light meal. Children tend to love it; back in the car it may take adults a while to shake off the feeling they've been time-warped.

You might want to stop for lunch or dinner before beginning your return trip. Good choices include **The Common Man** in Lincoln, popular with locals, or for authentic Italian, try Lincoln's **Fratello's Italian Grille**. Then, return to Manchester by heading south on I-93.

IN THE AREA

Accommodations

Bartlett Inn, Route 302, Bartlett. Phone: 1-800-292-2353; www.bartlett inn.com. A short ride from the Kancamagus Highway with a choice of large or small rooms and cottages. Inexpensive to moderate.

Indian Head Resort, 664 Route 3, Lincoln. Phone: 1-800-343-8000; www.indianheadresort.com. Located near many activities for families. On-site entertainment for children in-season. Inexpensive to moderate.

North Conway Grand Hotel, 72 Common Court (behind Settlers Green Outlet Village), North Conway. Phone: 1-800-655-1452; www.northconway grand.com. Lots of amenities and a prime location for shoppers. Moderate.

Red Sleigh Inn, 191 Pollard Road, Lincoln. Phone: 603-745-8517; www.redsleighinn.com. A charming small bed & breakfast. Inexpensive to moderate.

The Wilderness Inn, 57 Main Street (Route 3), North Woodstock. Phone: 1-888-777-7813; www.thewildernessinn.com. A lovely small inn, known for its tasty breakfasts. Inexpensive to moderate.

Dining

Fratello's Italian Grille, Route 112, Kancamagus Highway (in Village Shoppes Mall), Lincoln. Phone: 603-745-2022; www.fratellos.com. Excellent Italian food. Open for lunch and dinner. Moderate.

Horsefeathers, 2679 White Mountain Highway, North Conway. Phone: 603-356-2687; www.horsefeathers.com. Very popular and a local favorite since 1976, Horsefeathers' large menu makes it a good stop for families. More than the usual number of vegetarian choices, too. Open for breakfast, lunch, and dinner. Moderate.

Mountainside Restaurant, North Conway Grand Hotel, 72 Common Court (Route 16, behind Settlers Green Outlet Village), North Conway. Phone: 603-356-9300; www.northconwaygrand.com. Open for breakfast, lunch, and dinner. Moderate.

The Common Man, 10 Pollard Road, Lincoln. Phone: 603-745-3463; www.thecman.com. Open for dinner. New England comfort food and more. Moderate.

Attractions and Recreation

Clark's Trading Post, 110 Route 3, Lincoln. Phone: 603-745-8913; www .clarkstradingpost.com. Fees are all-inclusive for attractions. Bear shows begin the weekend of Memorial Day. Summer hours, 9:30–6; check website for hours during other seasons. Ages 6–64, $18; 65 and over, $16; 3–5, $7; under 3, free.

Loon Mountain Recreation Area, 64 Loon Mountain Road, Lincoln. Phone: 1-800-229-Loon; www.loonmountain.com. Skiing in winter; beginning in late June, you can try out a zip line, ride a gondola for beautiful views of the mountains, arrange for horseback or mountain bike rides, or try your luck on a climbing wall. Call or check website for seasonal activities and rates.

Russell-Colbath House, Passaconaway Historic Site, Kancamagus Highway. For details on open hours, check at the Saco Ranger Station in Conway or call 603-447-5448, ext. 0. Usually open May–Sept. with costumed

A scenic overlook in the town of Lincoln

interpreters; if closed, you can still wander the grounds, gardens, and cemetery. Admission free; donations appreciated.

Shopping

Settlers Green Outlet Village, 2 Common Court (Route 16), North Conway. Phone: 1-888-667-9636; www.settlersgreen.com. Open year-round.

Other Contacts

Saco Ranger Station, 33 Kancamagus Highway, Conway. Phone: 603-447-5448, ext. 0; www.fs.fed.us/r9/forests/white_mountain/contact. An all-day pass allowing you to leave your car in designated parking areas along the Kancamagus is $3. Station has restrooms, maps, and a small display of souvenirs and travel supplies. Open daily 8–4:30.

A renovated gas pump is among the finds at Lee Circle Antiques.

CHAPTER

8

New Hampshire: Antique Alley

Estimated length: About 30 miles from Manchester to the Lee traffic circle (or rotary) at Routes 4 and 125. Antique Alley stretches for about 22 miles; add an additional 40–50 miles for side trips.

Estimated time: Allow 45 minutes to travel from Manchester to the Lee traffic circle to start the tour. From there it's up to you whether to visit some or all of the antiques shops that you'll encounter and whether you choose to take some side trips. Plan at least an afternoon (some shops may not open until late morning).

Getting there: From Manchester take I-93 South to Exit 7, Route 101. Then take Route 101 East to Exit 7, Route 125, and turn left on Route 125 to the Lee traffic circle.

Highlights: This is a short tour that can be stretched out indefinitely if you are a devoted antiquer. For everyone else who just wants to take a peek at several **antiques shops** located conveniently near each other, the trip makes a good day trip or afternoon excursion. Allow additional time if you'd like to make a side trip to the **University of New Hampshire** campus, hike in the **Northwood Meadows State Park,** or take in a festival or the **Deerfield Fair** while you're in the area. Some antiques shops along this route are open all year; others may be closed or have limited hours in winter, so be sure to call or check the shops' websites just before you visit. Note, too, that although the shops are located in small towns in a quiet part of New Hampshire, most lie along Route 4, a busy through route from Portsmouth to Concord. For that reason you may find this trip is a good choice for a Saturday or Sunday drive when traffic is lighter.

Prepare for your trip by bringing plenty of cash, which may make haggling a bit easier. (Knowing that New Hampshire is one of a handful of states with no sales tax makes shopping easier as well!) Leave large handbags or backpacks in the car, however, as many shops have signs posted asking that you not bring them inside. Be sure to pick up an Antique Alley brochure at your first stop for information about some of the stores along the route, which winds through the towns of Lee, Northwood, Epsom, and Chichester.

Your first stop will probably be **Lee Circle Antiques**. You'll spot it easily on Route 125, just east of the traffic circle, especially if one of the shop's eye-catching, refurbished gasoline pumps is on display in front of the building. Although gas pumps may not be on your personal shopping list, judging from the apparent turnover, they're on someone's. Inside, you'll find a nice assortment of furniture, decorative items, and other small antiques including some attractive clocks.

If you don't mind a brief detour before you continue the antiques search, you may want to drive to nearby Nottingham to do another kind of shopping at the charming **Jenness Farm**. To get there, turn left off Route 4 to Garland Road, about 7 miles west of the Lee traffic circle. The specialty here is goat milk soaps and other personal and household products made with goat milk, herbs, lavender, and other natural products. The stars of the show are the adorable goats themselves, especially the newborn kids. In the spring, the farm often holds an open house to let visitors ooh and ahh over the newest baby goats and piglets. Any youngsters traveling with you will be thoroughly enchanted.

When you're ready to continue along Antique Alley, just keep going on Route 4. Many shops are multi-dealerships, so there can be upwards of five hundred individual dealers displaying their wares along Antique Alley on any given day. It's impossible to cover them all, but the following are a few suggestions to get you started. Don't hesitate, however, to stop at as many others as you can along the way—the route has many more shops than are listed on the official Antique Alley brochure. Take time to check

NEW HAMPSHIRE'S STATE UNIVERSITY

If you'd like to stroll through art galleries or perhaps take in a play or sports event, or if you happen to have a high school student with you who's beginning the college search, drive over to Durham to see what's happening at the University of New Hampshire. To reach it, head east from the Lee traffic circle on Route 4 for 2.5 miles, then turn right onto Route 155 and drive 2 miles to UNH. The quintessential New England college campus is one of the country's most beautiful. The centerpiece of the campus is the exquisite Thompson Hall, itself an antiques-lovers delight. Built in 1892 and now listed on the National Register of Historic Places, T-Hall, as it is known to generations of students, has beautiful architectural lines and a magnificent clock tower topped with a weathervane. Chimes in the tower ring daily across the campus and the small town of Durham that surrounds it. Opened in 1868 as the New Hampshire College of Agriculture and Mechanical Arts, it became the University of New Hampshire in 1923 and today enrolls some thirteen thousand undergraduate and graduate students. Watch for signs to the visitors center if you're interested in what's taking place on campus while you're in the area.

Thompson Hall at the center of the campus of the University of New Hampshire

Newmarket, just a few minutes' drive from Durham on Route 108 South, can be a good place to base yourself while you explore Antique Alley. The lovely **Three Chimneys Inn**, listed on the National Register of Historic Places, was built in 1649 and its **ffrost Sawyer Tavern** (that's not a typo; in the 1800s the homestead was owned by one ffrost Sawyer) serves excellent New England fare.

Antiques and collectibles fill the shelves at T. Berries Antiques and Primitives on Antique Alley in Northwood.

out the buildings the shops are housed in. Some are historic while others are colorful and downright funky. The shops are interspersed among vintage private homes, many of them dating from the 1700s and displaying the date they were built.

In Northwood, **R. S. Butler's Trading Company** is a good stop if you're interested in Victoriana, architectural salvage, and odds and ends like old records. Housed in a 3,600-ft., two-story barn, browsing here could keep you busy for hours. Also in Northwood, **T. Berries Antiques and Primitives** has a charming mix of antiques, including some nice early pieces, tasteful collectibles, and lovely locally made furniture. If you're a serious antiquer, you'll like the side-by-side shops of **Parker-French Antique Center,** with 135 dealers, and **Parker-French West Antique Center,** with 150 dealers. Both carry nice jewelry, glass, china, and primitives, and no reproductions or crafts. They are popular spots and the inventory turns over quickly, so there's always something new to find. Continue on to **Coveway Corner Antiques,** where much of the inventory comes directly from New Hampshire estates. The eclectic offerings including a nice selection of smalls and nautical items, along with furniture and primitives.

Because good eateries along Antique Alley are limited, you may want to stop in Northwood at **Johnson's Dairy Bar**, which despite its name serves excellent meals along with the enormous ice cream cones that bring locals here in droves in the summer. And if you're getting antiqued out by now, this may be a good time to relax at **Northwood Meadows State Park**, off Route 4 just before the Parker-French Antique Center. You won't find forest rangers, campsites, or interpretive trail markers here, but you will find almost 675 acres of wilderness that includes

DEERFIELD FAIR

Fall is a wonderful season for antiquing, so you may find yourself at Antique Alley during the time of the annual Deerfield Fair, which begins in late September. Started in 1876 as a way of uplifting Deerfield citizens' spirits after the railroad passed them by and their hopes of being named the state capital faded away, the fair is now the largest in New Hampshire. Just about everything you could want in a fair is here: tractor pulls, livestock exhibits, handiwork, musical events, a fiddle contest, a pig scramble, and a midway. It's a day of old-fashioned fun for the whole family. To reach the fairgrounds, take Route 107 South from Route 4 in Northwood. After 9.5 miles, turn left onto Route 43 for about 0.5 mile.

A tranquil pond at Northwood Meadows State Park

wetlands and a pond where you can launch a canoe or a kayak if you happen to have one with you. The trails are easy walking, even for children. You may pass another hiker or two or a few local residents walking their dogs, but much of the time it will be just you and the woods and birds singing in the trees. If you've brought along a picnic, there are a few picnic tables scattered around, constituting the sum total of the park's amenities. It's a lovely, pristine area in an unexpected location. No vehicles are allowed on the grounds, which adds to the peace and quiet, but there is ample parking space just outside the park entrance.

Continue on into **Epsom**, where you'll find **The Betty House**, four buildings crammed full of old tools, furniture, and trunks. Although the **Valley Artisans Craft Cooperative** does not sell antiques, the juried craft co-op does carry a wide variety of pottery, folk art–influenced painted items, jewelry, candles, quilts, and just about anything else clever people can create, as well as maple syrup products and locally made jams and jellies. You'll also find the **Circle Restaurant** in Epsom, where you can indulge in traditional New England cooking to round out your day. To get there from Route 4, take Route 28 south at the Epsom traffic circle and watch for the restaurant on the right.

Finish up your tour in **Chichester**. The many dealers at **Austin's Antiques** specialize in wonderful country furniture, pewter, and blown glass. Next door, **Keepers** specializes in Americana and authentic folk art, with an inventory that changes monthly.

If you're like most visitors to Antique Alley, you'll leave with visions of redecorating dancing in your head as you continue west on Route 4 and take I-93 South to return to Manchester.

IN THE AREA

Accommodations

Northwood Motel, Route 4, Northwood. Phone: 603-942-5476; www .northwoodmotel.net. Basic motel in the heart of Antique Alley. Very inexpensive.

Three Chimneys Inn, 17 Newmarket Road, Durham. Phone: 1-888-399-9777; www.threechimneysinn.com. Because the inn is near the University of New Hampshire campus, it may be booked well in advance for special events like homecoming, parents' weekend, and commencement. Moderate.

Dining

Circle Restaurant, 935 Suncook Valley Highway, Epsom. Phone: 603-736-8169; www.circlerestaurant.net. New England cooking including pot roast, seafood, and old-fashioned desserts. Open daily for breakfast, lunch, and dinner. Inexpensive.

Johnson's Dairy Bar, 1334 First NH Turnpike (Route 4), Northwood. Phone: 603-942-7300; www.eatatjohnsons.com. Open daily for lunch and dinner. Inexpensive.

Three Chimneys Inn, 17 Newmarket Road, Durham. Phone: 1-888-399-9777; www.threechimneysinn.com. The ffrost Sawyer Tavern and a seasonal outdoor terrace are open to the public for lunch (Tues.–Sat.) and dinner (nightly) and specialize in New England cooking. Antiquers will love the enormous hearth, Indian shutters, and wide plank floors. Moderate.

Attractions and Recreation

Deerfield Fair, Deerfield Fairgrounds, Route 43, Deerfield. Phone: 603-463-7214; www.deerfieldfair.com. Usually begins in late Sept.; check website for exact dates. Reduced-rate advance tickets available in many area stores; $10 at the gate, children under 12, free.

Jenness Farm, 77 Garland Road, Nottingham. Phone: 603-942-8051; www.jennessfarm.com. Open Wed.–Sun., 10–6, and every day from Thanksgiving to Christmas.

Northwood Meadows State Park, off Route 4, Northwood. Phone: 603-485-2034; http://nhstateparks.com/northwood.html. This is a wilderness area with no amenities. Open year-round. No fee.

University of New Hampshire, Durham. Many art, music, sports, and other campus events are open to the public. Phone: 603-862-1234; www.unh.edu.

Shopping

Austin's Antiques, 114 Dover Road, Chichester. Phone: 603-798-3116; www.nhantiquealley.com/AustinsAntiques.htm. Open daily, 9–4.

Coveway Corner Antiques, 1557 First NH Turnpike (Route 4), Northwood. Phone: 603-942-7500; www.nhantiquealley.com/CovewayCorner Antiques.htm. Open daily, 10–5.

Keepers, 114 Dover Road, Chichester. Phone: 603-798-3399; www .keepersantiques.biz. Open Wed.–Sat., 9–4, and Sun., noon–4.

Lee Circle Antiques, 83 Calef Highway (Route 125), Lee. Phone: 603-868-3424; www.nhantiquealley.com/LeeCircleAntiques.htm. Open Feb.–Oct., daily 10–5; Nov.–Jan., daily 10–4; closed Jan. 1–14.

Parker-French Antique Center, 1182 First NH Turnpike (Route 4), Northwood. Phone: 603-942-8852; www.nhantiquealley.com/Parker FrenchAntiqueCenter.htm. Open daily, 10–5.

Parker-French West Antique Center, 1190 First NH Turnpike (Route 4), Northwood. Phone: 603-942-5153; www.nhantiquealley.com/Parker FrenchWestAntiqueCenter.htm. Open daily, 10–5.

R. S. Butler's Trading Company, 102 First NH Turnpike (Route 4), Northwood. Phone: 603-942-8210; www.nhantiquealley.com/RSButlers TradingCompany.htm. Open Apr.–Nov., daily except Tues., 10–5. From Dec.–Mar., open weekends 10–5 and by appointment.

T. Berries Antiques and Primitives, 224 First NH Turnpike (Route 4), Northwood. Phone: 603-724-2184. Open year-round; call to confirm hours.

The Betty House, 105 North Road, Epsom. Phone: 603-736-9087; www .nhantiquealley.com/TheBettyHouse.htm. Open by appointment or by chance.

Valley Artisans Craft Cooperative, 10 Goboro Road, Epsom. Phone: 603-736-8200; www.valleyartisansnh.com. Open May–Dec., Wed.–Sun., 10–6, with extended hours over the winter holidays.

The Ottauquechee River flows through Quechee Gorge.

CHAPTER

9

Vermont:
Quechee and Beyond

Estimated length: About 55 miles from Montpelier to Quechee. About 100 miles to tour the area.

Estimated time: About one hour from Montpelier to Quechee. Allow time for antiquing, shopping, or other pursuits. A weekend is perfect.

Getting there: From Montpelier take I-89 South to Exit 1, then Route 4 West.

Highlights: On this trip you'll pass covered bridges, waterfalls, family farms silhouetted against a backdrop of tree-covered mountains, gurgling streams, and village greens. You'll travel along a portion of Vermont's scenic Route 100, which stretches the length of the state. Along the way, you'll visit dramatic **Quechee Gorge**, visit scenic **Woodstock**, shop for maple syrup in rustic country stores, and pick up the makings for a picnic lunch at a farmer's market. You'll want to allow a full weekend. And you'll wish you could stay longer.

One of Vermont's most popular tourist areas, **Quechee** can be very busy in the peak summer months and during foliage season. But despite the crowds—which often can be avoided if you start out early in the morning—there are two attractions you won't want to miss. The first, **Quechee**

Gorge, was formed some thirteen thousand years ago and is sometimes referred to as Vermont's Little Grand Canyon—and yes, calling it even a small Grand Canyon is a bit of a stretch, since the depth of the Grand Canyon is 1 mile and Quechee Gorge is about 163 feet deep. Nevertheless, Quechee Gorge is pristinely beautiful and well worth a visit.

You can simply stop at pull-offs along Route 4 for a quick look, but better still is the walk into the gorge from the **Quechee Gorge Visitor Center,** a downhill hike right to the water over a smooth, well-maintained 0.5-mile trail cut through a forest of pines and hemlocks. (Just remember that a walk downhill means a walk uphill on the return trip, and as with any trail, weather conditions can make things muddy or slick. Check at the visitor center if you have any concerns about trail conditions.) The gorge takes its name from the river, which the indigenous Abenaki called Ottauquechee, or "waters of the chasm." For about one hundred years, the river and falls powered a very successful woolen mill. The development of **Quechee State Park,** which encompasses the gorge, began almost immediately after the mill closed in 1952. You'll understand why it is now one of Vermont's most popular state parks when you breathe in the pine-scented air, hear birds chattering overhead, and enjoy the wildflowers and clear water of the Ottauquechee.

If you'd like to do some canoeing, kayaking, or fishing, **Wilderness Trails** can fix you up with everything you need, whether you're a family looking for a quiet paddle on the Ottauquechee or a more adventurous trip on the White River just north of Quechee Village.

The second must-see attraction lies just west of Quechee Gorge on Route 4. The **Vermont Institute of Natural Science Nature Center (VINS)** is home to many eagles, owls, hawks, and other raptors, all of which have sustained injuries that make it impossible to return them to the wild. At

---

NO, NOT *THAT* WOODSTOCK

Travelers sometimes confuse Woodstock, Vermont, with a New York town that gave its name to the famous 1969 Woodstock rock festival (actually held in Bethel, New York). Max Yasgur's farm, where music history was made, is some 250 miles from this Woodstock, so no tie-dyed T-shirts are needed. There are, however, plenty of musical events in and around town. Just watch the local newspapers for concerts and groups performing in the area or check out the Town Crier Board on Elm Street to find out what's happening while you're here.

VINS they are well cared for and provide an opportunity for observation and study. The site also has pleasant gardens and nature trails open to the public.

Quechee is also home to **Simon Pearce**, located just beyond Quechee Gorge in a former mill overlooking a rushing waterfall on the Ottau-quechee. To get there, turn right on Waterman Hill Road, then left onto Quechee Main Street. At Simon Pearce, you can watch glassblowers and potters at work creating the glassware and decorative items that have made the company famous, and then have lunch or dinner in the adjoining restaurant. Plan your visit around a glassblowing workshop if you can, because you'll enjoy the whole process of seeing molten glass being transformed into high-end stemware and graceful accent pieces.

BALLOONS OVER QUECHEE

If you happen to be in Quechee in mid-June, you'll enjoy the annual Quechee Hot Air Balloon, Music, and Craft Festival. Hot air balloon pilots come from all over to participate and offer rides. In addition, there are craft displays, food and drink vendors, and live entertainment for all ages.

You might want to base yourself in Quechee at the **Quechee Inn,** whose windows offer stunning views of the river. Or, if you'd like to shop till you drop, **Quechee Gorge Village**, easily reached on Route 4, awaits. About 12 businesses are clustered here, so you can find everything from Vermont cheese at the **Cabot Quechee Store**, to lovely pewter at **Danforth Pewter**, to antiques at the **Vermont Antique Mall**, Vermont's largest antiques center. The funky **Farmers Diner** here has won lots of accolades for serving excellent meals from locally sourced products.

When you're ready, continue on Route 4 West to **Woodstock**. Take one picturesque village green and surround it with sturdy Federal houses. Add nearby art galleries, shops, and chummy restaurants where

MORE COWS THAN PEOPLE?

It has often been said that Vermont has more cows than people, but in fact the state has the largest *ratio* of cows to people in the country. Currently there are about 150,000 cows and 621,800 people in the state. Black and white Holsteins are the most prevalent bovines, but you'll also see lots of brown Jersey cows with big, soulful eyes.

locals, seeing you pondering a map, bring over their coffee and plop down to help, and you have the essence of Woodstock. Its best asset may be that

Downtown Woodstock

despite being achingly beautiful—a national magazine called it the prettiest small town in America—there's nothing cloying about the village. Woodstock has what New Englanders call character. Settled more than two hundred years ago by farmers and tradesmen, Woodstock was a quiet country village until it was discovered by professionals who brought more wealth into the area and built many of the homes that make Woodstock so architecturally enchanting.

Many visitors come to Woodstock to stay at the popular **Woodstock Inn & Resort**, a destination in itself with a midtown location overlooking the village green that can't be beat. The inn's amenities include tranquil gardens, a fabulous new spa, and a nearby golf course and fitness center. The overall ambiance at the resort is one of laid-back elegance, with no one taking themselves too seriously. This philosophy was obvious during a recent visit with a snowstorm raging outside. A fire was roaring in the huge lobby fireplace when a wedding party arrived. The bride took her vows in a designer wedding gown—accessorized with white fur-lined boots. The Inn's friendly tavern is always buzzing (besides drinks, there's also a small bar menu) and the **Red Rooster** dining room offers classy fare from a chef and servers who know their stuff.

American history buffs may be interested in a neat bit of trivia: Woodstock is home to five bells cast in the Paul Revere foundry—the most Paul Revere bells in any one location in the country—one of which is on a pedestal on the grounds at the Woodstock Inn. Another used to hang in the belfry of the Congregational Church on Elm Street. It's now on a small porch beside the church, and visitors are welcome to stop by to admire and touch this bit of Americana.

On the village green, just across the street from the Woodstock Inn, you'll find a farmer's market in full swing every Wednesday afternoon during the summer months. It's one of many you'll come across as you tour the area, all good places to pick up homemade snacks or picnic items and, in many cases, Vermont-made jewelry and crafts. There's also an information booth on the green if you'd like help planning your stay. Nearby, Woodstock's **Middle Bridge** spans the Ottauquechee River as it flows through the village. Built in 1969, Middle Bridge is not an old-timer as covered bridges go, but it's photogenic nonetheless.

Downtown you'll find **F. H. Gillingham & Sons.** Picturesque, and purveyors of a little bit of everything in the best tradition of old-time country stores—of which there are many in the Woodstock area—Gillingham's has been in the same family for more than 125 years.

SNOW TIME

The popular sport of snowboarding got its start in Vermont, with the first national championships held in 1982 near Woodstock. Skiing, of course, has long been popular here, with the country's first rope tow put in place in 1934.

From downtown Woodstock, take Route 12 North to the **Marsh-Billings-Rockefeller National Historical Park** and **Billings Farm and Museum.** The 550-acre park takes its name from the early environmentalists and conservationists who nurtured the property. The first was environmentalist George Perkins Marsh, author of *Man and Nature,* who grew up here. Marsh sold it to railroad entrepreneur Frederick Billings, an admirer of Marsh's conservation efforts. The park has 20 miles of walking

Vegetables are piled high at the Woodstock Farmers' Market.

trails and carriage roads; architecture or garden buffs will want to tour the lovely mansion and its grounds, originally built for the Marsh family and updated by Billings and, later, by his granddaughter, Mary French Rockefeller, and her husband, Laurance Rockefeller.

In 1871 Billings established a working dairy farm on the property, with the goal of developing a model for future generations to emulate. The farm remains today thanks to the Rockefellers, who were determined to carry on the legacy of both Marsh and Billings.

The Billings Farm and Museum is a working museum dedicated to conservation and Vermont's agrarian history. You can visit the 1890 farmhouse, but the highlight for most visitors is seeing the cows, sheep, oxen, and other farm animals and attending the programs ranging from talks on land management to early New England cooking.

The special summer events are fun, too. You might celebrate the Fourth of July here by listening to a reading of the Declaration of Independence, making silhouettes, participating in an old-fashioned spelling bee, and churning ice cream. Or you might arrive on Antique Tractor Day or a day devoted to a celebration of Vermont's cows. National Park Service rangers offer a 2-mile walk that acquaints visitors with the park's role in the Civil War. A pasture on the property served as a training ground for local troops. Woodstock's population at the time was about 3,000; ultimately it lost 39 men in the war. The tour offers a poignant look at the war from the home-front perspective of a small New England town.

Next, head west out of Woodstock on Route 4 to see an especially interesting covered bridge. The 134-ft. **Lincoln Bridge** is about 3 miles outside the village. Built in 1877, its arched truss is the only one of its kind in the country.

You can take a break at this point, have a bite to eat, and check your e-mail at the friendly **Woodbridge Café & Coffeehouse** just a couple of miles up the road. When you're ready to roll, continue on through a num-

---

BACK TO THE PEOPLE

A side trip to Plymouth Notch, south on Route 100A from Bridgewater Corners, takes you to the **President Calvin Coolidge State Historic Site**, boyhood home of the 30th president. Vice President Coolidge assumed the presidency on August 3, 1923, upon the death of President Warren Harding. Coolidge was visiting his father when word arrived of Harding's death, and the senior Coolidge, a notary public, administered the oath of office by candlelight in the middle of the night. Legend has it that the senior Coolidge later admitted he had no idea whether he was legally empowered to swear in his son. Perhaps Yankee common sense prevailed and the Coolidges simply decided to get the job done without a lot of fuss.

A visit to the Coolidge homestead gives a good sense of the president's Vermont upbringing, the same background that gave him a reputation for being both frugal and reticent and earned him the nickname Silent Cal. Several buildings comprise the site, including Coolidge's birthplace attached to a general store, the larger home across the street where he spent his childhood from age four, and the one-room schoolhouse he attended through eighth grade. He is buried in a cemetery on the grounds, fulfilling his comment upon leaving the presidency: "We draw our Presidents from the people...I came from them and I wish to be one of them again."

The Lincoln Covered Bridge

ber of picturesque villages, including Bridgewater Corners, home of the **Long Trail Brewery**. Brewmasters here have developed some interesting German-style beers and ales, so if you're interested in the science of suds, plan a stop.

Enjoy the beauty of Vermont's Green Mountains as you continue along Route 4/100 toward Killington; then turn right on Route 100 toward **Rochester**. Stop if you wish, at small stands selling maple syrup and crafts, or check out antiques for sale on someone's front porch. Many of Vermont's dairy farms are along this drive, and you'll see plenty of bemused cows watching the tourists watching them.

The **Rochester Ranger Station** on Route 100, about 2 miles north of Rochester, is a good stop for information and brochures about the area. Right next door is **Sunshine Valley Berry Farm** where you can pick—or just pick up—berries of all kinds in-season, maple syrup, jam, and other goodies.

For a scenic side trip, turn left onto Route 125 in Hancock to enjoy a setting of farms, mountains, old cemeteries, lush greenery in summer, and spectacular foliage in the fall. The road winds through the **Green Mountain National Forest,** and you'll find a convenient pull-off for some of the best picture taking of your trip. When you're sated with scenery, retrace your steps to Route 100 and continue on to Granville and Warren, turning right at the sign to Warren Village, where you'll find the **Lincoln Gap Covered Bridge**. Built in 1879 with an interesting and unusual overhang, the 62-ft. bridge spans the Mad River.

Back on Route 100, continue on to **Waitsfield,** an excellent stopping point for a meal at the **East Street Café**. At the **General Wait House and Visitors' Center,** you can find out about special events in this area. Just be sure to bring some small change with you. The human staff does all the work, but the real boss of the office is an irresistible cat named Yoda who charges five cents a pat, with all proceeds going to the local humane society.

> ### A LONG AND WINDING ROAD
>
> Vermont's **Long Trail** is a long-distance (272 miles) hiking trail extending the length of the state, from the Massachusetts' border to Canada. The oldest such trail in the country—it inspired the Appalachian Trail—hiking it requires physical stamina, experience, and the right equipment, since it meanders through boggy areas, past ponds, and over most of the major peaks in the Green Mountains. Completed in 1930, the trail has about 70 basic shelters available to hikers.

Great Vermont-made crafts await you nearby at the **Artisans' Gallery** on Bridge Street and the **Mad River Glass Gallery** on Route 100. Leaving Waitsfield, you'll bear right on Route 100B toward Middlesex, passing bright red barns with white roofs just begging to be photographed against their background of thickly forested hills.

All good things come to an end, and you'll be reluctant to leave this corner of Vermont. But when you must, turn left onto Route 2 and then head south on I-89 if you want to return to Quechee. To return to Montpelier, turn right on Route 2 and travel about 8 miles.

IN THE AREA

Accommodations

Quechee Inn, 1119 Quechee Main Street, Quechee. Phone: 1-800-235-3133; www.quecheeinn.com. The inn combines early 19th-century character with every modern convenience in a tranquil farm atmosphere. Inexpensive to moderate; includes breakfast.

HOW SWEET IT IS

Imagine the surprise of European settlers when friendly Native Americans showed them that liquid from certain trees could be boiled down to a tasty sweet syrup or boiled even longer to produce sugar. It must have been a pleasant change after a diet of mostly bland and starchy food. If you're traveling in Vermont in late February or March, watch for sugar shacks, where you can observe the boiling process—called "sugaring off"—and for public pancake breakfasts where the focus is not so much on the food as it is on what gets poured over it.

The process of sugaring off to produce all that maple syrup is a lengthy one. Forty gallons of sap must be boiled down to make one gallon of syrup. Each maple tree yields just 10 gallons of sap in an average season—meaning that gallon of syrup you buy to bring home is the yield of four trees.

Waitsfield Inn, 5257 Main Street, Waitsfield. Phone: 1-800-758-3801; www.waitsfieldinn.com. Built in 1825, the historic inn has been thoroughly updated with all modern amenities. Great downtown location. Pub and restaurant on the premises. Inexpensive; rates include breakfast.

Woodstock Inn & Resort, 14 The Green, Woodstock. Phone: 1-800-448-7900; www.woodstockinn.com. Expensive; rates include complimentary shuttle to the resort's golf course and racquet and fitness center and free admission to the Billings Farm & Museum.

Dining

Easy Street Café and Restaurant, Route 100, Waitsfield. Phone: 802-496-7234; easystreetmarket.com. Open for breakfast, lunch, and dinner. A sure sign of a friendly and efficient restaurant is that when you call to tell them you left your jacket behind, they offer to mail it—and it reaches home before you do. All that and good food, too! Inexpensive.

Quechee Inn, 1119 Quechee Main Street, Quechee. Phone: 1-800-235-3133; www.quecheeinn.com. Dinner only; reservations recommended. Moderate.

Red Rooster at the Woodstock Inn & Resort, 14 The Green, Woodstock. Phone: 1-800-448-7900; www.woodstockinn.com. Open daily for lunch

A waterfall cascades beside Route 100, just north of Granville.

and dinner. Thoughtful wine list, excellent cuisine and service. Reservations are a good idea. Moderate to expensive; unusually good children's menu.

Simon Pearce, 1760 Quechee Main Street, Quechee. Phone: 802-295-1470; www.simonpearce.com. Open daily for lunch and dinner; Sunday brunch; seasonal terrace menu. Moderate.

The Farmers Diner, Quechee Gorge Village, Route 4, Quechee. Phone: 802-295-4600; www.farmersdiner.com. Open for breakfast and lunch. Inexpensive to moderate.

Woodbridge Cafe & Coffeehouse, 531 Woodstock Road (Route 4), Woodstock. Phone: 802-332-6075; www.woodbridgecoffehouse.com. Open for breakfast, lunch, and dinner. Vermont specialties. Free wi-fi. Inexpensive.

Attractions and Recreation

Artisans' Gallery, Bridge Street, Waitsfield. Phone: 802-496-6256; www .vtartisansgallery.com. A variety of handmade items and artwork by Vermont artists and artisans.

Long Trail Brewing Company, Junction of Routes 4 and 100A, Bridgewater Corners. Phone: 802-672-5011; www.longtrail.com. Self-guided tours available. Open daily, 10–7; pub grub served 11–6. Inexpensive.

Mad River Glass Gallery, 4237 Main Street (Route 100), Waitsfield. Phone: 802-496-9388; www.madriverglassgallery.com. Specializes in blown and sculptural glass. Open daily.

Marsh-Billings-Rockefeller National Historical Park and Billings Farm and Museum, Route 12 and River Road, Woodstock. Phone (park and mansion): 802-457-3368, ext 22; www.nps.gov/mabi. Open Memorial Day weekend through Oct. 31. Mansion tours: Adults, $8; seniors, $4; children 15 and younger, free. Civil War Walking Tour offered occasionally during the summer. Phone (Billings Farm and Museum) 802-457-2355; www. billingsfarm.org. Open May 1–Oct. 31, 10–5; in Nov.–Feb., open weekends, 10–3:30. Adults, $12; seniors, $11; children 5-15, $6; ages 3-4, $3. Two-day combination tickets for museum and farm: Adults 16-61, $17; seniors, $13.

The Town Green in Rochester

President Calvin Coolidge State Historic Site, 3780 Route 100A, Plymouth Notch. Phone: 802-672-3773; www.historicvermont.org/coolidge. Open late May to mid-Oct., daily, 9:30-5:30. Admission : Adults, $7.50; ages 6–14, $2; under 6, free.

Quechee Balloon Festival. Phone: 800-295-5451; www.quecheeballoon festival.com. Held annually in June on the Village Green Circle on Main Street. Adults, $10; children 6–12, $5; ages 5 and under, free. Ticket is good for the entire weekend; festival usually kicks off on Friday afternoon.

Quechee Gorge at Quechee State Park. Gorge and surrounding park are located on Route 4, Quechee; official park address is 764 Dewey Mills Road, White River Junction (about 7 miles from Quechee). Phone: 802-295-2990; www.vtstateparks.com/htm/quechee.htm. Open 10–9 Memorial Day weekend through Oct. 19, 10–9 (or sunset). Free admission to Gorge; fees for camping.

Quechee Gorge Visitor Center, Route 4, Quechee, 2 miles from the intersection of I-89 and Route 4. Phone: 802-295-6852. Open daily except holidays, 9–5.

Simon Pearce, 1760 Quechee Main Street, Quechee. Phone: 802-295-2711; www.simonpearce.com. Glassblowing workshops, Mon.–Tues., 9–5 and Wed.–Sun., 9-9; pottery workshops, Sat.–Sun., 9–4.

Vermont Institute of Natural Science Nature Center (VINS), 6565 Woodstock Road, Quechee. Phone: 802-359-5000; www.vinsweb.org. Open May Oct., daily, 9 5:30. Admission: Adults, $10.50; seniors, $9.50; ages 4-17, $8.50; ages 3 and under free.

Shopping

Cabot Quechee Store, Quechee Gorge Village, Route 4, Quechee. Phone: 1-888-792-2268; www.cabotcheese.com. Cheeses, wines, beer, and Vermont specialty products. Open daily.

Danforth Pewter, Quechee Gorge Village, Route 4, Quechee. Phone: 1-800-222-3142, Ext. 249; www.danforthpewter.com. Beautiful pewter gifts, decorative items, and jewelry. Open daily.

F. H. Gillingham & Sons, 16 Elm Street, Woodstock. Phone: 1-800-344-6668; www.gillinghams.com. A little bit of everything, from maple syrup to books, classic kids' toys, kitchen utensils, and gadgets for everyone. Open daily.

Sunshine Valley Berry Farm, 129 Ranger Road (Route 100), Rochester. Phone: 802-767-3989; www.vermontberries.com. Organic berries and other Vermont products. Open July 4–Columbus Day.

Vermont Antique Mall, Quechee Gorge Village, Route 4, Quechee. Phone: 1-800-438-5565, Ext. 108; www.quecheegorge.com/vermont -antique-mall.php. About 450 booths offer a wide variety of antiques and collectibles. Flea market every Sun., May–Oct.

Other Contacts

General Wait House and Visitors Center, Mad River Valley Chamber of Commerce, Route 100, Waitsfield. Phone: 1-800-82-VISIT; www.mad rivervalley.com.

Rochester Ranger Station, 99 Ranger Road (Route 100), Rochester. Phone: 802-767-4261; www.fs.fed.us/r9/forests/greenmountain/htm /greenmountain/g_contact.htm. Open Mon.–Fri., 8-4:30; and also on Sat. from May 29–Oct.9.

Wilderness Trails, c/o Marty Banak, 1119 Quechee Main Street, Quechee. Phone: 802-295-7620; www.wildernesstrailsvt.com. Canoe and kayak rentals, fly-fishing, excursions for all levels of ability.

The Battle of Bennington Monument and statue of Colonel Seth Warner of the Green Mountain Boys

CHAPTER

10

Vermont: Bennington to Brattleboro on the Molly Stark Byway

Estimated length: About 120 miles from Montpelier to Bennington. The Molly Stark Byway is 48 miles long.

Estimated time: About two and a half hours from Montpelier to Bennington. You can drive the byway in two hours or less, but with so much to see, try to allow a leisurely half day.

Getting there: From Montpelier take I-89 South to Exit 3. Then head west on route 107 for about 13 miles to Route 100, continuing south about 10 miles to Route 4 West. After about 11 miles, turn onto Route 7 South into Bennington.

Highlights: This short but pretty drive takes you through the heart of southern Vermont. You'll enjoy sweeping views of the **Green Mountains,** working farms, historic monuments and sites, and **covered bridges.** Come in the early spring for the first maple syrup, or in the fall for glorious foliage. And if you come in June, you just might catch a parade of flower-bedecked cows!

You'll know you're approaching Bennington when you see the **Bennington Battle Monument** jutting more than 306 feet into the air. Built between 1887 and 1891 of magnesian limestone, this tallest manmade structure in Vermont honors the important Revolutionary War battle of 1777 that Bennington commemorates each year on August 16. The battle itself really took place a few miles from Bennington in what is now New York State, but the monument is erected on a former storage site for military supplies that played an important role in the conflict.

Running low on provisions after a long siege of fighting, it seems that British general John Burgoyne (known as "Gentleman Johnny" because he was always kind to his troops) decided to raid the Colonists' supply depot and sent an army of some seven hundred men to see what they could pilfer. Getting word of their approach, Vermonters appealed to neighboring New Hampshire for help, and soon a combined force of Vermonters, New Hampshire militia, and a few troops from Berkshire County, Massachusetts, readied themselves for battle. The two thousand New Englanders were under the command of General John Stark. (For more about General Stark, see Chapter 6.) The Colonial forces waylaid the advancing British about 5 miles northwest of Bennington, but just when it seemed that victory was theirs, additional British troops arrived and the fighting began anew. The battle turned again in favor of the Colonists thanks to the timely arrival of a unit of Green Mountain Boys under the command of Colonel Seth Warner. The Colonists' success in keeping needed supplies out of the hands of the British helped turn the tide of the war, with Burgoyne surrendering all his forces a few weeks later.

The Bennington Battle Monument is open to visitors, who are greeted

---

THE GREEN MOUNTAIN BOYS

Organized in 1770 as an unauthorized militia, the group that became known two years later as the Green Mountain Boys is an integral part of Vermont history. They even carried their own flag—a dark green field to represent their name, with a canton or top inner corner of blue sprinkled with thirteen white stars representing the thirteen colonies. Under the fiery leadership of Ethan Allen, the militia's goal was to protect the interests of area farmers and other settlers who had received land grants from New Hampshire to property located in what we now know as Vermont. At the time, however, New York laid claim to the same land and disputed New Hampshire's right to grant it to anyone. The squabbles continued for years, with Allen and his men laying the groundwork for the eventual separation of Vermont from both New Hampshire and New York, a goal finally achieved in 1791 when Vermont became the 14th state to join the union. The Green Mountain Boys also participated in many key battles of the Revolutionary War, including their vital role in helping to win the Battle of Bennington.

at the entrance by a diorama depicting one of the battle engagements. Nearby, an enormous iron kettle is thought to have been used by General Burgoyne's troops. The site of the former supply depot also has a monument to General Stark and the New Hampshire men who fought in the battle, a bronze statue of General Stark, a monument to Colonel Warner, and other memorials. To reach the site from downtown Bennington, follow Route 9 West and take a sharp right onto Monument Avenue.

Periodic events and reenactments take place to commemorate the Battle of Bennington. The **Bennington Area Visitors' Center** on Route 7, just before you come into the downtown area, will have listings for these and other activities taking place during the time of your visit.

If you'd like a bite to eat before you continue on, try the **Blue Benn Diner** downtown, an authentic 1940s railroad car–style diner complete with handwritten menu specials posted on the walls.

The **Bennington Museum** on Route 9 was originally opened to house artifacts commemorating the Battle of Bennington. Today it displays both changing and permanent exhibits of paintings and sculpture by Vermont artists, as well as Vermont-made furniture and the world's largest collection of Bennington pottery. In addition, an unexpected and charming wildflower trail loops behind the museum.

A highlight for many museum visitors is viewing the largest public collection of works by Grandma Moses and seeing the schoolhouse she attended as a child. Although often associated with Vermont because of the primitive New England scenes she loved to paint, Grandma Moses (Anna Mary Robertson, 1860–1961) was actually born just across the border in New York State and spent most of her life there. When she began to paint in earnest at age 76, her lighthearted, colorful works resonated with admirers across the country who appreciated her simple style and the happy country nostalgia of her paintings. She was a friend of Norman Rockwell, who lived in Arlington, Vermont, not far from her home in Eagle Bridge, New York.

This is just one of several interesting museums in town. The **Vermont Covered Bridge Museum** is a great place to learn more about Vermont's covered bridges in general and several in and around Bennington in particular. It's located at the **Bennington Center for the Arts**, itself a fascinating repository of Native American crafts, masterful bird carvings, and other art.

If you'd like to get out on the water, **BattenKill Canoe** can set you up with everything you need for a couple of hours of exploration on your own or for a tour with other paddlers. If you prefer to fish the Battenkill River,

ROBERT FROST'S VERMONT

There's a lot of distance between war and poetry in every sense of the word, but just a short side trip from Bennington will bring you to South Shaftsbury, where fans of Robert Frost should stop at the **Robert Frost Stone House Museum.** The poet lived in the house for a while in the 1920s, and readers of his poetry will appreciate the ways in which his surroundings influenced his work, including "Stopping by Woods on a Snowy Evening" (which, strangely enough, was written in June). The home and weathered barn are surrounded by the stone walls and

The Robert Frost Stone House Museum in South Shaftsbury; its surroundings are thought to have inspired many of Frost's poems.

birch and other trees that played such important roles in his works. To get there from downtown Bennington, take Route 7 North for 3miles to the exit for Route 7A into South Shaftsbury.

Back in Bennington, you can visit Frost's grave behind the historic 1806 **Old First Church** on Route 7. "I had a lover's quarrel with the world," reads the epitaph on his flat gravestone, often decorated with flowers and poetry by his admirers, while the poignant farewell of his wife, Elinor, reads, "Together Wing to Wing and Oar to Oar." The graveyard also contains the remains of American, British, and Hessian (German mercenaries who fought with the British) troops who fell at the Battle of Bennington.

considered by many to be the country's premier trout-fishing river, the **Battenkill Angler** can get you started or help you hone your skills.

Back on the road, you may find yourself passed by antique cars whose drivers are making a pilgrimage to the **Hemmings Motor News Filling Station** on Main Street. You can fill up here, then browse the antique cars and assorted memorabilia on display in the museum and store. Each year in mid-September, Bennington hosts antique and classic car fans from across the country at the **Bennington Car Show and Swap Meet**.

Artists, craftspeople, and potters have long been inspired by the changing seasons and quiet life among the hills of Vermont. **Bennington Pottery**, in business since 1948, has become well known for its durable, beautiful pottery, ranging from baking dishes to coffee cups and huge pasta bowls. Stores across the state carry its products, but you can visit one of the pottery's own retail stores, **Potters Yard Factory Store,** in downtown Bennington.

There's also good shopping at **Camelot Village**, where you'll find an antiques center with more than 140 dealers, crafts, a country store, and shops selling other items such as candles and vintage fashions.

Leaving Bennington, take Route 9 East, the 48-mile **Molly Stark Byway**, through the Green Mountain National Forest. Along the way you'll notice a series of colorful obelisks obviously designed in the style of the Bennington Battle Monument. There are eight of these in all, each giving a brief history of the byway along with little nuggets of local lore. You'll learn, for example, that tollgates once collected money from travelers on this same route, charging $1 for a four-horse stagecoach, fifty cents for four-wheeled vehicles, and a penny each "for sheep and swine."

Obelisks like this one along the Molly Stark Byway in Wilmington provide anecdotes and historical information.

COVERED BRIDGES

Some of Vermont's most beautiful covered bridges are all within a short drive, so fire up the camera and plan to visit five of them during one easily driven tour. Start with the **Henry Bridge** by heading north on Route 7 for 1.2 miles. Turn left on Route 7A, and after 1 mile, bear left on Route 67A. After about 2 miles, turn left onto River Road. The Henry Bridge crosses the gurgling Walloomsac River, and nearby is a tranquil place to stay overnight, the 1769 **Henry House,** where a big front porch overlooks the peaceful scene.

To find the **Paper Mill Bridge**, go back 1 mile on Route 67A and turn right onto Murphy Road. To visit the **Silk Bridge,** continue on Route 67A for another 0.5 mile and turn right onto Silk Road. These bridges also span the Walloomsac.

If you're willing to drive a bit farther afield, head back to Route 7 and drive north 12 miles to Exit 3, then follow Route 313 West for 8 miles to the **West Arlington Bridge.** Spanning the Battenkill River, not only is the bridge among the prettiest you'll ever see, in-season kayakers and canoeists drift beneath it, making for terrific photo opportunities. The bridge is near the home of the late artist Norman Rockwell, now the **Inn on Covered Bridge Green**, a popular bed & breakfast.

Your final stop will be the handsome **Chiselville Bridge** over Roaring Branch Brook, named for an old chisel factory that once stood nearby. From the West Arlington Bridge, go back 4.4 miles on Route 313, turn left onto East Arlington Road, and continue for 2 miles until you reach the bridge.

The Henry Covered Bridge

Theories abound as to why some bridges were covered, one of the most prevalent being that blocking the view of rushing water kept horses and other animals calmer when crossing the bridge. The real reason, however, is simply that covering the wooden trusses protected the bridges from the weather and made them last longer. Although certainly not in the plans of the original designers, romantic purposes are also served by New England's covered bridges, being popular secluded places in which to propose, to conduct small wedding ceremonies, or to gather for wedding photos.

By the late 19th century there were some 10,000 covered bridges scattered throughout the country. Today about 750 authentic covered bridges remain in the United States, with more than 100 located in Vermont, where forests provided plenty of wood to build them in abundance. If it's a bridge, and it's covered, it's not necessarily an authentic covered bridge, however. That designation goes only to those bridges built with a deck, a cover, and wooden trusses. Unlike covered bridges in some other parts of the country where the entrances, or portals, were sometimes elaborate, showcasing the builder's talents, New England's covered bridges tend to be simple and utilitarian, in keeping with the area's traditional no-nonsense lifestyle.

Few people realize that covered bridges are also home to a variety of wildlife. Stand quietly just inside a covered bridge and you may see phoebes, who are particularly fond of nesting in them. Many return to the same bridge year after year. Barn swallows swoop through, catching insects as they go. Bats and insects often take up residence in covered bridges, and you may see an owl or other raptor peering down at you from the rafters.

Many covered bridges in Vermont and elsewhere in New England are painted red—not to make for stunning photo opportunities, although that's a happy result—but because in days gone by ochre was an inexpensive and readily available pigment. Mixed with milk, turpentine, and other ingredients, the paint proved to be surprisingly durable.

This route is dotted with charming little pull-offs, shops selling antiques or maple sugar products, and a handful of restaurants. Roughly halfway between Bennington and Brattleboro, **Dot's Restaurant** in Wilmington shouldn't be missed. Located in a historic 1832 building, Dot's serves up some of the best road food you'll come across in your travels. If you'd prefer to picnic or just want to walk around for a bit, **Molly Stark State Park** has pretty open lawns, thick woods, and picnic areas along with hiking trails.

The byway ends at the bustling town of **Brattleboro** in the Connecticut River Valley. **The Brattleboro Museum and Art Center** is home to world-class contemporary art exhibits that have ranged from avant-garde paintings to horse sculptures. In addition, the museum is a cultural center, hosting author readings and other events.

No matter what the weather, the citizens of Brattleboro know how to put on a good celebration. **Brattleboro Winter Carnival**, established in 1957, takes place over a period of several days. If you happen to be visiting in winter, this old-fashioned event featuring sugar on snow (hot maple syrup poured over snow to make a sort of toffee almost guaranteed to remove your fillings), a carnival queen pageant, a chili cook-off, pancake breakfasts, and sleigh rides involves much of the community and is nostalgic fun for visitors.

Come June, Brattleboro honors the cows of Vermont during the **Strolling of the Heifers**. Sporting bright flower garlands, heifers (female cows that haven't yet born a calf) saunter along at the head of a parade that also includes cows, bulls, goats, and other farm animals, along with tractors, decorated floats, and marching bands. A weekend-long festival follows. It's a cheerful family event that helps kick off summer.

You've probably passed a number of potteries during your drive, but if you're still looking to bring home a piece of Vermont, you may find what you want at **Brattleboro Clayworks** on Putney Road (Route 5). This is a cooperatively managed clay studio and retail store where you can find a vari-

---

WHO WAS MOLLY STARK?

Route 9, the Molly Stark Byway, was named for the wife of General Stark of Battle of Bennington fame. Supposedly, when the general saw the advancing enemy, he rallied his men by saying, "There are the Red Coats! They will be ours tonight or Molly Stark sleeps a widow!" The byway is thought to mark the route General Stark took when he and his troops marched home after their successful battle.

As for Molly herself, from the little that is known about her she seems to have been the antithesis of a demure Colonial wife, apparently being possessed of an iron will and a constitution to match. In addition to bearing eleven children, she worked tirelessly to encourage young men to join the militia. When a smallpox epidemic broke out among her husband's troops, she nursed as many as she could back to health. And as the Battle of Bennington raged on, she turned an outbuilding on the family homestead into a makeshift hospital where she treated both American and enemy wounded.

The Brattleboro Museum and Art Center, noted for its horse sculptures

ety of artists' interpretations of bowls, teapots, storage containers, ceramic tiles, and decorative items. Visitors are welcome to watch the artists at work.

One of the most unusual places to stay in Brattleboro is the art deco **Latchis Hotel & Theatre**, where you can book a hotel room and watch a movie or attend a special concert in one of several theaters, all under one roof. Brattleboro has a number of restaurants including **The New England House** on Route 9, or you can pick up goodies to go at the **Vermont Country Deli**.

THE JUNGLES OF VERMONT?

In the 1890s, author Rudyard Kipling lived in a cottage near Brattleboro while writing the stories that would eventually be incorporated into *The Jungle Book*. Later, he built a large home nearby.

To return to Montpelier, take Route 5 South one mile to I-91 North. Go to Exit 10, then take I-89 North to Exit 8 Montpelier.

IN THE AREA

Accommodations

Four Chimneys Inn, Route 9 (1 mile west of Route 7), Bennington. Phone: 802-447-3500; www.fourchimneys.com. A charming country inn. Wide range of room rates; check website for details.

LEAF PEEPING

Vermont's spectacular fall foliage attracts leaf peepers from all over the country and the world, all hoping to arrive during the elusive "peak" of color. While it's impossible to predict the peak color until it's almost there—much depends on the temperature and rainfall of the previous spring and summer—a trip planned between the last week of September through mid-October should guarantee some satisfactory sightings. From mid-October on, colors will begin to fade and the leaves will gradually fall from the trees.

What causes this annual phenomenon? As days grow shorter and the sunlight necessary to manufacture chlorophyll lessens, the leaves of maple trees lose their green color and—some years quickly, some years more gradually—turn to blazing shades of yellow, orange, and crimson. It's a sight that has inspired generations of artists and poets and is all the more beautiful because it is so elusive and so fleeting. The Vermont Foliage Hotline (802-828-3239) can help you target the peak season in the Bennington-Brattleboro area or wherever else your travels take you within the state.

Henry House Inn, 1338 Murphy Road, North Bennington. Phone: 1-888-442-7045; www.henryhouseinn.com. History abounds in this 1769 house, once the home of a soldier in the Battle of Bennington. Inexpensive; includes continental breakfast.

Inn on Covered Bridge Green, 3587 River Road, Arlington. Phone: 1-800-726-9480; www.coveredbridgegreen.com. Fans of Norman Rockwell should not miss the opportunity to stay in the very home where he painted some of his most famous works. Moderate; includes a bountiful breakfast.

Latchis Hotel & Theatre, 50 Main Street, Brattleboro. Phone: 802-254-6300; www.latchis.com. Convenient downtown location. Inexpensive to moderate.

Dining

Blue Benn Diner, 314 North Street, Bennington. Phone: 802-442-5140. All the traditional diner comfort foods, plus more contemporary dishes. Open Wed.–Fri., for breakfast, lunch, and dinner; closes Mon. and Tues. at 5 and on Sat. and Sun. at 4. Inexpensive.

Dot's, 3 East Main Street, Wilmington. Phone: 802-464-7284; www.dots ofvermont.com. Popular with locals. Try the award-winning chili. Open for breakfast, lunch, and dinner. Inexpensive.

Four Chimneys Inn, Route 9 (1 mile west of Route 7), Bennington. Phone: 802-447-3500; www.fourchimneys.com. Dinner only. Moderate to expensive.

The New England House, 254 Marlboro Road (Route 9), Brattleboro. Phone: 802-254-6886; www.thenewenglandhouse.com. Open for lunch and dinner; closed Mon. and Tues. Inexpensive to moderate.

Vermont Country Deli, 436 Western Ave. (Route 9), Brattleboro. Phone: 802-257-9254; www.vermontcountrydeli.com. Vermont products, gourmet picnic items. You can't dine in at the deli, but it's a great stop for picnic items. Open daily 7–7. Moderate.

Contented cows watch the passersby.

Attractions and Recreation

Bennington Battle Monument and State Historic Site, Monument Avenue, Bennington. Phone: 802-447-0550; www.historicvermont.org /sites. Open mid-Apr.–Oct. 31. Admission: Adults, $2; children 6–14, $1; ages 5 and under, free.

Bennington Car Show and Swap Meet, Green Mountain Racetrack, Route 7, Pownal. Phone: 802-447-3311, Ext. 14; www.benningtoncarshow .com. Held annually for several days in mid-September for lovers of antique and classic cars. Vendors sell everything related to the hobby. Tractor pulls, entertainment, food tents, and a flea market. Admission, $8; under 12, free.

Bennington Center for the Arts and Vermont Covered Bridge Museum, Route 9 West at Gypsy Lane, Bennington. Phone: 802-442-7158; www.benningtoncenterforthearts.org. Open daily except Sun., 10–5. Admission charged.

Bennington Museum, Route 9, Bennington. Phone: 802-447-1571; www.benningtonmuseum.org. Open daily except Wed., 10–5; in Sept. and Oct., open daily. Closed in Jan. Admission: Adults, $10; seniors and students over 18, $9; under 18, free. Wildflower trail is free to all.

Brattleboro Museum and Art Center, 10 Vernon Street, Brattleboro. Phone: 802-257-0124; www.brattleboromuseum.org. Open Thurs.–Mon., 11–5; closed on major holidays. Admission: Adults, $6; seniors, $4; students, $3; ages 5 and under, free.

Brattleboro Winter Carnival. Information: www.brattleborowinter carnival.com.

Hemmings Motor News Filling Station, 216 Main Street, Bennington. Fill your tank, grab a snack, and relish the cars of yesteryear.

Molly Stark State Park, 705 Route 9 East, Wilmington. Phone: 802-464-5460; www.vtstateparks.com/htm/mollystark.htm. There is a hiking trail up 2,154-ft. Mount Olga. Open Memorial Day weekend through Columbus Day weekend, 10–sunset.

Robert Frost Stone House Museum, 121 Route 7A, South Shaftsbury. Phone: 802-447-6200; www.frostfriends.org. Open May–Nov., daily except Mon., 10–5. Admission charged.

Strolling of the Heifers, Main Street, Brattleboro. Information: www.strollingoftheheifers.com.

Shopping

Brattleboro Clayworks, 532 Putney Road, Brattleboro (about 1.5 miles north of Brattleboro center on Route 5). Phone; 802-254-9174; www .brattleboroclayworks.com. Gallery and store open Fri.–Sat., 10–5.

Camelot Village, Route 9 West, Bennington. Phone; 802-447-0039; www.shopsatcamelotvillage.com. Open daily 9:30–5:30.

Potters Yard Factory Store (Bennington Pottery), 324 County Street, Bennington. Phone: 1-800-205-8033; www.benningtonpotters.com. Open daily 9:30–6, except Sun. 10–5.

Other Contacts

Battenkill Angler, 6204 Main Street, Manchester Center. Phone: 802-379-1444; www.battenkillangler.com. A full-service guide operation for those wanting to try their luck fishing for trout in the Battenkill River. Rates vary; see website for details.

BattenKill Canoe, Ltd., Route 7A, midway between Arlington and Manchester. Phone: 1-800-421-5268; www.battenkill.com. Open May 1–Nov.1 for rentals and tours. Rates vary by trip; see website for details.

Bennington Area Chamber of Commerce Visitors' Center, Route 7, Bennington. Phone: 1-800-229-0252; www.bennington.com. Open year-round, Mon.–Fri., 9–5 and Sat. 9–4. Also open Sun. 10–4 from mid-May through mid-Oct.

Molly Stark Byway information: www.mollystarkbyway.org.

This sign in Prospect Harbor is a reminder of the sardine harvesting and canning industry that once flourished along the Maine coast.

CHAPTER

11

Maine: The Schoodic Peninsula and Down East

Estimated length: Portland to Ellsworth is about 150 miles, plus about 155 miles to tour Down East villages and the Schoodic Peninsula.

Estimated time: Allow three and a half hours from Portland to Ellsworth, plus a minimum of a day to drive through the area and two to three days to thoroughly explore the small coastal towns.

Getting there: From Portland, Maine, take I-295 North to Brunswick, then travel Route 1 North to Ellsworth.

Highlights: Tiny villages dot the Maine coast and its islands, but for a look at traditional fishing communities not gentrified for summer tourists, there may be no better place to explore than the Schoodic Peninsula, with its picturesque fishing villages like **Winter Harbor** and **Corea**. Although located just a few miles from the well-known attractions of busy Bar Harbor, the peninsula remains one of Maine's best-kept secrets. Few travelers realize that the Schoodic Peninsula is also home to a pocket-sized piece of **Acadia National Park**, just as scenic and much less busy than the main portion of the park on nearby Mount Desert Island. But now *you* know...

Lumber trucks rumbling past as you near the town of **Ellsworth** on Route 1 are a reminder that Maine's vast woods lie just to the north. Between you and wilderness, however, are many of the state's most photogenic coastal villages. For most people, the best time to travel here is late spring through mid-October. Many attractions, restaurants, and hotels open sometime between mid-May and Memorial Day weekend and close after Columbus Day, and those that do stay open in winter may have shortened hours. Still, winter has its own stark beauty in this part of Maine, especially when a snowfall dusts rooftops, and slanted sunlight sparkles on the cold, gray-blue water of the bays. Come here during the coldest months and any illusions you may have about the glamorous life of Maine lobstermen will be put to rest when you see ice-covered boats and crews returning from their labors in the fading light of a midwinter afternoon.

Ellsworth, the gateway to Down East Maine, is the site of the **Woodlawn Museum,** also known as the Col. Black Mansion, on Route 172 a short distance from Route 1. Fans of historic homes know that they are often furnished with pieces "typical of the era" but not original to the house. Not so at Woodlawn, which was left to Ellsworth with all its furnishings intact, right down to the Black family's reading material and glassware. The Federal-style home and the carriage house containing the family's sleighs and horse-drawn carriages were completed in 1827 for Col. John Black, one of the first entrepreneurs to recognize that great wealth could be made from the Maine woods. He used his fortune made from lumbering to build a magnificent mansion on 180 acres of land; two other generations of Blacks lived here before the colonel's grandson deeded the home to the town. The grounds are a popular place for walking, and the Ellsworth Antiques Show, the longest-running summer antiques show in the country, is held here around the middle of August.

Ellsworth is also home to **Birdsacre** and the **Stanwood Wildlife Sanctuary** on Route 3. Birdsacre, the restored residence of ornithologist and wildlife photographer Cordelia Stanwood (1865–1958), gives a peek into the life of a complicated and sometimes anguished woman who devoted fifty years of her life to studying, documenting, and photographing the birds around her in an era when women were not always recognized for their intellectual achievements. A 200-acre wildlife sanctuary surrounds her home, a must stop for anyone interested in hawks, owls, and other birds.

Back on Route 1, **Helen's** offers plenty of meal choices from a down-home menu. Save room for a huge slice of one of Helen's famous pies—large enough to share—or do as some local devotees of Helen's do and eat

The start of the Schoodic National Scenic Byway near Ellsworth

the whole piece yourself, wash it down with a cup of coffee, and call it lunch.

About nine miles beyond Ellsworth, a large inscribed boulder on the left marks the beginning of the **Schoodic National Scenic Byway.** Drive another 4 miles and take a quick detour off the byway by turning right on Route 185 and heading into **Sorrento** for your first peek at a working fishing village, home to about three hundred residents. Like many points of land that jut out from Maine's rocky coast, this was once a summer gathering place for local Native American tribes.

You'll pass bays dotted with evergreen-covered islands and the buildings of the Sorrento Lobster Pound, where huge trucks are usually parked outside, ready to carry the lobsters to market. Out on the water, lobster boats come and go near the gated pound area, where harvested lobsters are kept alive before being packed for shipping. On a clear day, Mount Desert Island is visible in the distance.

Head back on Route 185 to Route 1, then travel 5 miles to Route 186 and drive south to the Schoodic Peninsula, traveling through the small villages of West Gouldsboro and South Gouldsboro into **Winter Harbor.** Fans who remember the television program *Murder, She Wrote* may think

Inner Harbor in the town of Winter Harbor

they've arrived in Cabot Cove when they pass by the island-filled harbors and get a look at the village (population about one thousand). On Main Street the town doctor's shingle hangs across the street from the **Winter Harbor 5&10.** Inside this old-fashioned dimestore you'll find everything from table lamps and toys to nail polish and planters, sweatshirts and batteries. Take time to wander through the aisles to find something you didn't realize you needed. For a special gift or souvenir from Maine, check out nearby **Blair Art Glass** for attractive tableware and decorative items.

To have lunch with the locals, head for **Chase's Restaurant** for home-style cooking, including plenty of fresh seafood. A more upscale option in-season is **Fisherman's Inn Restaurant,** noted both for its excellent seafood and a surprisingly eclectic menu. Goodies for a picnic or a snack of pastries and coffee can be gathered up at **J. M. Gerrish Provisions.**

If you're traveling in Winter Harbor the second Saturday in August, be sure to attend the **Winter Harbor Lobster Festival**, which includes lobster-boat races (a year's bragging rights go to the winning captain, whose feat is no small one since lobster boats are built more for durability than speed), road races, a parade, and of course, all the fresh-from-the-ocean lobsters you can eat.

Winter Harbor is a good place to stay overnight, especially if you'd like to scoot over to Bar Harbor on the seasonal ferry the next day to visit this much-better-known part of Down East Maine, with its many attractions—and many tourists.

The eye-catching stone building on Chapel Lane is **Channing Chapel**, with an interesting history all its own. In 1887 a summer resident named David Flint announced his intention to build a Unitarian house of worship using local labor. That winter, townspeople lugged fieldstones to the site, having used their Yankee smarts to determine that such heavy labor would be much easier in colder weather. The chapel was ready for use by late summer 1888, complete with two ornate windows, one dedicated to Flint and the other to William Ellery Channing, the founder of Unitarianism. At Flint's direction, a portion of the building was set aside as a small library to house classic tomes. In 1958 the building was given to Winter Harbor by the Unitarian Association and later a preservation society was formed to maintain the building. The lovely stone chapel is now home to the **Winter Harbor Public Library.**

Before leaving Winter Harbor, take in the postcard-perfect open-ocean view from **Grindstone Point**, reached by turning left off Main Street onto Grindstone Road. Among the islands clearly visible from here are Ned Island and Turtle Island, just two of the thousands of small islands off the coast of Maine.

Many travelers find it hard to leave Winter Harbor—it's that kind of place—but when it's time to travel on, turn east on Route 186 and follow the signs to **Acadia National Park** to enjoy a 6-mile, one-way loop of the only portion of the park on the mainland (the rest of the park is located on Mount Desert Island, Isle au Haut, and a few tiny islands off the Schoodic Peninsula). Follow the one-way traffic signs and adhere to the park rules, including no camping or feeding wildlife. If Fido is traveling with you, he is welcome but must be leashed. It's important to leave the park as pristine as you find it, so carry trash out with you and do not remove rocks or flowers.

Enjoying this lovely part of Acadia is a very different experience from visiting the equally beautiful but very busy main part of the park on Mount Desert. Usually uncrowded, especially in the spring and fall, there are plenty of pull-offs along the loop road to pause for picture taking or just to enjoy the 2,366 acres of pristine scenery. The parking area at about the halfway point offers a view of the open ocean and the rocky coast. In some places, boiling magma has pushed up through the granite bedrock, then cooled and hardened to form abstract streaks called black dikes.

Along the shoreline you'll be rewarded with glimpses of starfish, sea urchins, and other creatures. Overhead, or perched along the shore, are terns, black guillemots, ducks, cormorants, and a variety of gulls. As you explore, be sure to stay well away from the surf. Tempting as it may be to get close to the water, even on a calm day rogue waves, those huge, unforeseen waves that come in quickly and wash everything in their path out to sea, are a fact of life along the Maine coast.

When you can tear yourself away, continue the loop and take a right onto Route 186 toward **Prospect Harbor**, until recently the home of the last remaining sardine canning factory in Maine. Prospect Harbor marks the end of the Schoodic National Scenic Byway, but you can turn right off Route 186 onto Route 195 and drive 3 miles to **Corea**, perhaps the quietest little fishing village in the area. Photographers will find wonderful possibilities in the piled-up lobster traps, fishing and lobstering boats, and the craggy faces of men and women who earn their living from the sea.

A bright blue building on Corea Road is the uniquely named **Old Good Goods** and worth a stop for anyone who enjoys moseying around antiques shops.

HOW ACADIA GOT ITS NAME

In 1524, while exploring the area we now know as Down East Maine, the Italian explorer Giovanni Verrazano is said to have been struck by the similarity of the coastline to the Greek region of Arcadia. Over time, the spelling was changed slightly and Acadia was adopted as the name of what is now the nation's tenth-most-visited national park.

If you're not yet sated with scenery and rustic villages, leave the Schoodic Peninsula on Route 186 and turn right onto Route 1, traveling north toward Machias. The road passes through several typical Down East villages, including **Cherryfield**. Although named for the wild cherries that once grew along the Narraguagus River, it's the acres of low-bush blueberry barrens throughout this area that now make Cherryfield famous as the blueberry capital of the world. Each September this little village of about eleven hundred residents celebrates the blueberry with a two-day festival that includes a pancake breakfast, road races, fireworks, and a chicken barbecue. Cherryfield's historic district includes a number of lovely old homes lining the river, most dating from the mid-18th to late 19th centuries.

Continue toward Machias through **Harrington**, home to **Worcester Wreath Company,** where the Arlington Wreath Project was born in 1992 when owner Merrill Worcester quietly donated five thousand Christmas wreaths to mark graves at Arlington National Cemetery. Word got out about his project in 2005 when a poignant photo of the decorated graves appeared on the Internet. Subsequent requests for wreaths at other veterans' cemeteries resulted in **Wreaths Across America,** an annual movement that delivers balsam wreaths every December to veterans' cemeteries in every state. Worcester Wreath is the world's largest producer of holiday balsam decorations, and some of its buildings, including one topped with a big red bow and looking much like a gift package, are visible from Route 1.

For a tour of an interesting historic home, visit the **Ruggles House** in the quiet country village of **Columbia Falls**. Furnished with many family artifacts, the Federal-style home was built in 1820 for Thomas Ruggles, who made his fortune exporting lumber. Built by housewright Aaron Sherman and woodcarver Alvah Peterson, the home is noted for its unusual design and the beauty of its intricate hand-carved trim and flying staircase.

Just after Columbia Falls, turn right onto Route 187 toward **Jonesport.** If time allows, take a boat tour out to **Machias Seal Island** to see the largest

---

BRINGING THE BLUES

Maine's Native Americans are credited with being the first to recognize blueberries' versatility, using them to flavor food and probably for medicinal purposes as well. Native Americans may have taken their cue from the state's black bears after seeing them rake through the bushes with their claws in search of a sweet treat. Maine's 60,000 acres of blueberry barrens turn pale pink and white in the spring when the bushes bloom, blue in August and September at harvest time, and crimson in winter. Commercial harvesting began in the late 1840s and now produces some 88.5 million pounds of blueberries a year. With the recent widespread acknowledgment of their antioxidant and other health benefits, blueberries now have a multimillion-dollar effect on the state's economy. Many individuals and families continue a long Maine tradition of picking small quantities of blueberries to sell from roadside stands.

Jonesport's Sawyer Memorial Congregational Church, with its tall steeple, is typical of churches found throughout New England.

group of Atlantic puffins in Maine. With their compact, torpedo-shaped bodies, thick beaks—bright orange edged with blue during the breeding season—and propensity for flying at top speed just above the water, they are sometimes called the parrots of the ocean. About three thousand Atlantic puffins live on Machias Seal Island, which is in Maine waters but jointly claimed by the United States and Canada. In 1832 Canada built the small lighthouse on the island and continues to maintain it.

In downtown Jonesport, the **Sawyer Memorial Congregational Church**, with its beautiful stained-glass windows, weathervane, and weathered steeple, is quintessential New England. Just across Sawyer Street is **Harbor House Inn**, a bed & breakfast and antiques shop and a convenient place to stay while touring the area.

Jonesport lies at the end of a peninsula connected by a bridge to **Beals Island**. So closely are the communities linked, both geographically and genealogically, they are usually referred to in one breath as Jonesportand-Beals. Many island families bear the surname Beals or Alley, and virtually every house along the narrow streets is home to a lobster fisherman and every cove filled with lobster boats. **Great Wass Island**, connected to the southern end of Beals, is a very different place, with 1,540 acres overseen by The Nature Conservancy. There's a small parking area where you can leave the car in order to hike, explore the rugged coastline with its lounging harbor seals, and watch for birds, including puffins, blue herons, osprey, and bald eagles. The island's peat bogs are thought to have formed some ten thousand years ago. Scraggly evergreens dominate Great Wass, but there is prettier vegetation, too, including a variety of unusual wildflowers.

Tall Barney's Restaurant awaits as soon as you cross the bridge back to Jonesport, a must-stop for immersing yourself in the culture of this seafaring village. With luck you may be invited to sit at the angled center table where the locals gather to tell tall tales and poke good-natured fun at tourists. Tall Barney's gets its name from a man named "Barna" Beal, born in 1835 in Jonesport. Barna grew to be six feet seven inches tall and three hundred pounds in an era when many people barely topped five feet. When a humorous poem about the man who had grown so huge that women hid their good chairs when he came calling appeared in a Maine newspaper, both Jonesport and Tall Barney had their moment of fame. Tall Barney's Restaurant is noted for excellent seafood, much of it locally harvested and all of it seasoned with a splash of dry humor. As the owners say on their

Beals Island harbor

website, "If you don't see it on the menu, just ask. We aim to please. Just ignore the screams from the kitchen."

Passing through the tiny community of **Jonesboro** (population about six hundred) you'll see signs for **Roque Bluffs State Park**, located about 6 miles south of Route 1. Here it's possible to alternate a swim in the freshwater pond with a dip in the ocean at Englishman Bay. A peaceful spot of more than 270 acres, the park has excellent views of Maine's rocky coast.

After viewing so much water, you may want to get out on it and enjoy a canoe trip on the Machias River. The river runs through **Machias**, the county seat, whose name means "bad little falls" in the Passamaquoddy language. There are indeed some rushing little falls close to the center of town, surrounded by a park. Guided canoe tours are available for those wanting to explore the river up close, a wonderful excursion on a hot summer day.

History was made in Machias on June 12, 1775, in what is now the **Burnham Tavern Museum**. Shortly after the battle of Lexington and Concord, Machias citizens found themselves staring at the guns of the British ship HMS *Margaretta,* whose commander, one Lt. Moore, demanded they start shipping lumber to Boston to aid the British war effort. Gathered in the Burnham Tavern taproom and faced with either assisting the enemy or the possible destruction of the town, the men ultimately decided to capture the lieutenant. But how? Ultimately it was decided to surround him as he prayed in church. But the wary commander saw them coming, jumped out a window, and made it to his ship, which immediately headed out into the ocean. Not to be thwarted, 40 brave men of Machias, armed with a couple of muskets and assorted pitchforks, hoes, and scythes, hopped into two merchant vessels and took off after him. They captured the ship and wounded Lt. Moore, who was brought back to a makeshift hospital in the tavern, where he ultimately died. The battle is remembered today as the first naval engagement of the American Revolution.

The gambrel-roof tavern, built in 1770, is a designated National Historic Site. It is furnished with period pieces, not least of which is a chest said to be stained with the blood of Lt. Moore.

A quiet place today, Machias's heydey was the early 19th century, when it was the second busiest lumber port in Maine. With a current population of about twenty-three hundred, it has more tourist facilities than some

---

LOBSTER TALES

By state law, Maine lobster fishermen may set up to eight hundred traps, but each lobstering area establishes its own strictly adhered-to limits. Each lobsterman's traps are marked with floating buoys in a distinctive color combination. One or more identical buoys mounted on each boat make it clear to other lobstermen that a boat is pulling its own traps. Legal lobsters in this state measure between three and a quarter and five inches from the eye socket to the start of the tail, which means that you won't find the Moby-Dick of lobsters on a menu anywhere in Maine. Legal lobsters are usually under five pounds. Egg-bearing females may not be kept. In some areas, lobstermen voluntarily notch a "V" into the tail of an egg-bearing female before returning it to the ocean. Lobstermen who catch a V-notched lobster without eggs will toss it back into the sea, knowing it is a breeder that will help sustain the lobster population.

Liberty Hall in Machiasport

of the smaller villages in the area. Among the best are the **Bluebird Motel** and the **Machias Motor Inn**, and **Helen's** and the **Bluebird Family Ranch Restaurant**, good stopping points for either overnight stays or a casual meal.

To explore neighboring **Machiasport**, head south on Route 92 to visit the Machiasport Historical Society, housed in the 1810 **Gates House** and 1850s **Cooper House.** The Gates House is filled with marine artifacts, and the Cooper House contains a replica of a 1910 post office, an early-20th-century schoolroom, and a collection of old tools. These buildings help preserve the history of this tiny town whose waters once were busy with cargo and passenger ships, including one that made a regular run from Boston to Bar Harbor to Machiasport.

Just across the street is ornate **Liberty Hall**, listed on the National Register of Historic Places and currently undergoing a full-scale restoration. Built in 1873, the hall served, at various times, as Machiasport's Town Hall and as a cultural and community center. The Italianate-style building, designed by local architect Andrew Gilson, overlooks the head of Machias Bay where the small band of Machias men captured the HMS *Margaretta.*

Also on Route 92 are a few earthen breastworks and other remnants of **Fort O'Brien**, which helped guard towns along the Machias River during the American Revolution, the War of 1812, and the Civil War. Built in 1775, the fort didn't last a year before being burned by the British. Refortified in 1776, it would again be burned by the British in 1814 and again be rebuilt shortly afterward. Check out "Napoleon," a cannon from the Civil War era, capable of firing a 12-pound cannonball across the river.

Take a few more minutes to continue down the road through Bucks Harbor and park at **Jasper Beach**, one of the most unusual beaches you'll come across anywhere. Having very little sand, the beach is made up almost entirely of large volcanic pebbles with red, blue, and other hues, all washed smooth and deposited by the tides. Apparently someone mistook the reddish stones for jasper, but they are really rhyolite. In sneakers or other sensible footwear you can easily walk along the beach and enjoy the view, which often includes soaring eagles overhead.

The end of the road comes at **Starboard,** a tiny village with pretty views that's home to a few fishing families. From Starboard return to Route 1 and head back to Ellsworth, where you can retrace your steps to Portland. Or, to travel on to a livelier side of Maine, take Route 3 from Ellsworth to Bar Harbor before heading home.

IN THE AREA

Accommodations

Black Duck B & B, Crowley Island Road, Corea. Phone: 207-963-2689; www.blackduck.com. Open May–Oct. Inexpensive to moderate.

Bluebird Motel, Route 1, Machias. Phone: 207-255-3332. Open year-round. Very inexpensive.

Harbor House on Sawyer Cove, 27 Sawyer Square, Jonesport. Phone: 207-497-5417; www.harborhs.com. A bed & breakfast inn and antiques and gift shop. Open year-round. Inexpensive.

Machias Motor Inn, Route 1, Machias. Phone: 207-255-4861; www .machiasmotorinn.com. Open year-round. Very inexpensive.

Oceanside Meadows Inn, Prospect Harbor Road, at the head of Sand Cove just before Acadia National Park at Schoodic. Phone: 207-963-5557; www.oceaninn.com. Inexpensive to moderate.

Dining

Bluebird Ranch Family Restaurant, 78 Main Street, Machias. Phone: 207-255-3351; www.bluebirdranchrestaurant.com. Open daily from 6 AM–8 PM; buffet breakfast and lunch on Sun. Frequent theme nights offer a good bargain. Inexpensive.

Chase's Restaurant, 193 Main Street, Winter Harbor. Phone: 207-963-7171. Opens at 7 AM year-round. Inexpensive.

Fisherman's Inn Restaurant, 7 Newman Street, Winter Harbor. Phone: 207-963-5585. Open mid-May through mid-Oct. Moderate.

Helen's, 55 Downeast Highway, Ellsworth. Phone: 207-667-2433. Inexpensive.

Helen's, Route 1, Machias. Once associated with Helen's in Ellsworth, Helen's of Machias, now under a different ownership, has also made its reputation on down-home cooking and spectacular pies. Phone: 207-255-

8423. Open year-round for breakfast, lunch, and dinner but hours vary; call to verify. Inexpensive to moderate.

J. M. Gerrish Provisions, 352 Main Street, Winter Harbor. Phone: 207-963-2727; www.jmgerrish.com. Open 8–5; deli, bakery, and picnic items. Inexpensive.

Tall Barney's, 52 Main Street, Jonesport. Phone: 207-497-2403; www.tall barneys.com. Seasonal hours; check website or call for details. Inexpensive to moderate.

Attractions and Recreation

Bar Harbor Ferry. Phone: 207-288-2984; www.barharborferry.com. From about June 23–Aug. 31 the ferry runs daily, making at least five round trips between Winter Harbor Marina and Bar Harbor. Adults, $29.50; children, $19.50; bikes, $6.

Birdsacre and Stanwood Wildlife Sanctuary, Route 3, Ellsworth. Phone: 207-667-8460; www.birdsacre.com. Birdsacre homestead open daily June–Sept., 10–4. Sanctuary open daily throughout the year from dawn to dusk. Free admission.

Burnham Tavern Museum, Route 192, Machias. Phone: 207-255-6930; www.burnhamtavern.com. Open mid-June through Sept., Mon-Sat., 9–4.

Channing Chapel/Winter Harbor Public Library, 18 Chapel Lane, Winter Harbor. Phone: 207-963-7556; www.winterharbor.lib.me.us. Open Wed., Fri., and Sat., 1:30–4.

Fort O'Brien, Route 92, Machiasport. Phone: 207-941-4014. Open Memorial Day through Labor Day.

Gates House and **Cooper House,** Route 92 South, Machiasport. Open early July to early Sept., 12:30–4:30. Free admission; donations appreciated.

Roque Bluffs State Park, 145 Schoppee Road, Roque Bluffs. Phone (in season): 207-255-3475. Changing rooms, picnic tables, and grills available. Open May 15 through Oct. 30. Small admission fee.

Ruggles House, 146 Main Street, Columbia Falls. Phone: 207-483-4637; www.ruggleshouse.org. Open June 1–Oct. 15. Guided tours Mon.–Sat., 9:30–4:30; Sun. 11–4:30. Adults, $5; children $2.

Winter Harbor Lobster Festival. For details: www.acadia-schoodic.org /lobsterfestival.html.

Woodlawn Museum, Surry Road (Route 172, about 0.25 mile from Route 1), Ellsworth. Phone: 207-667-8671; www.woodlawnmuseum.com. Tours of the mansion in May and Oct. daily from 1–4; from June–Sept. on Sat. 10–5 and Sun. 1–4. All tours begin on the hour. Admission: Adults, $10; children, $5; under 5, free. The museum grounds are open year-round from sunrise to sunset. Free admission; long walks and picnics encouraged!

Shopping

Blair Art Glass, 670 Newman Street, Winter Harbor. Phone: 207-963-2664.

Old Good Goods, 646 Corea Road, Corea. Phone: 207-963-2510.

Winter Harbor 5 & 10, 349 Main Street, Winter Harbor. Phone: 207-963-7927; www.winterharbor5and10.com. Along with selling a little bit of everything, the store will make copies, send faxes, and ship items home for you. Open daily 8:30–5 from May 1–Christmas; closed on Sun. the rest of the year.

Winter Harbor Lobster Co-op, 23 Pendleton Road, Winter Harbor. Phone: 207-963-5857; www.winterharborlobstercoop.com. Buy lobsters here or arrange to have them shipped home. The co-op's impressive website includes interviews with local lobster fisherman and interesting facts about lobstering as a way of life.

Other Contacts

Acadia National Park at Schoodic Peninsula: Contact: www.acadia -schoodic.org.

Cherryfield and its blueberry festival: Website: www.cherryfield.us.

Guided canoe trips of the Machias River (and others): Mike Patterson, Master Guide. Phone: 207-338-3932; www.wildsofmaine.com.

Norton of Jonesport, Jonesport. Provides trips to Machias Seal Island aboard the *Chief.* Advance reservations are a must. Exact early-morning departure time varies with sea and weather conditions; always confirm both place and time of departure with owners the night before. Tours run from the first week of June through mid-Aug., taking about 90 minutes each way and spending about two hours on the island. $100 per person. Phone: 207-497-2560 or 207-497-5933; www.machiassealisland.com.

The Nature Conservancy (information about Great Wass Island and other Maine sites): www.nature.org/maine.

Worcester Wreath Company and **Wreaths Across America:** www.worcesterwreath.com and wreathsacrossamerica.org.

A scale model of Saturn is part of the mini solar system built by the people of Aroostook County.

CHAPTER

12

Maine: Aroostook County

Estimated length: About 215 miles from Portland to Patten. This tour of the area is about 290 miles.

Estimated time: Allow three and a half hours from Portland to Patten. Aroostook County is a vast place, and to explore even the small portion of it described in this chapter, you should plan on a very full day, or better still, a weekend.

Getting there: From Portland take I-295 North to Gardiner, then I-95 North to Exit 264. Then take Route 11 North to Patten.

Highlights: To Mainers, it is simply "the County." Maine's Aroostook County comprises 6,453 square miles—about 21.6 percent of the state or the approximate size of Connecticut and Rhode Island combined—a large wilderness area dotted with small towns and traversed by thousands of miles of waterways. This is Maine at its most natural, with many residents living close to the land, hunting, fishing, hiking, camping, and enjoying its pristine beauty. It would take a book to write about all of Aroostook County, but this drive touches on a few places and events in the northern and eastern parts of the county that are of special interest to travelers. Among them are beautiful **Mount Katahdin,** picturesque **Eagle Lake,** an intriguing **Midsommar Fest,** and an **Acadian Village.** Allow a day or two if you can, because you'll want to pull over often for photographs of the spectacular scenery, along with visiting some of the area's other attractions. You'll be very close to Canada on this trip, so if you think you might want to cross the border, be sure to have your passport with you.

Descendants of early Native Americans who explored the forests and paddled the waterways of northern Maine continue to live in **Aroostook County** today. Many members of the Aroostook Band of Micmacs reside in Presque Isle and members of the Houlton Band of Maliseet live in the county seat at Houlton. They are two of five federally recognized tribes residing in Maine, which also include the Passamaquoddy Tribe of Indian Township in Princeton, the Passamaquoddy Tribe at Indian Point in Perry, and the Penobscot Nation in Old Town.

For the most part, the northern Maine tribes intermingled peacefully for generations. By the early 1500s, we know that the Micmacs were trading furs to white explorers. In time they began to turn away from their traditional summer fishing pursuits and concentrated on hunting as the demand for furs increased. Inevitably this led to less game being available, and some rancor developed among the tribes. Then border concerns began to arise after the arrival of permanent white settlers as the British and Americans clamored for clear ownership of large tracts of thickly forested land. In 1783 the Treaty of Paris ended the American Revolution but failed to establish a clear boundary between what were then British North America (specifically, today's New Brunswick, Canada) and northern Massachusetts (today's Maine). Resentment over the ill-defined border simmered for decades, increasing in 1820 when Maine separated from Massachusetts and wanted a final determination of where its border lay. In 1838 tension grew to the point that both sides sent armed military personnel to the border, the closest the ongoing arguments came to outright war. Fortunately, cooler heads prevailed, and in 1842 the Webster-Ashburton Treaty delineated the boundaries once and for all, satisfying the white settlers but giving little thought to the fact that the boundary ran through Indian territory and divided area tribes between the two countries. The boundary disputes went down in history as the "Aroostook War"—fortunately, a war that wasn't. Today, of course, New Bunswick and Maine residents have the best of relationships, crossing the border frequently for shopping, evenings out, and vacations. In addition, the Canadian and American border towns rush to each other's aid when there are fires or other emergencies.

Culturally, Aroostook County is an intriguing mix of descendants of New Brunswick and Nova Scotia families whose traditions reflect their French heritage, descendants of early British settlers, and Americans who have come from other parts of the country, lured by the county's sheer size and opportunities for rural life. Many travelers are surprised to find a small but active Swedish population here in remote Aroostook County.

The 2000 census measured the county's population at about seventy-four thousand, so with 6,453 square miles to choose from, there are plenty of opportunities to live as remotely as one wishes. As you might expect in an area of cultural diversity and very long winters, residents of the County have found plenty of reasons to establish festivals and fairs and have become known for snow-sport events that bring participants and visitors to the area from all over the country.

Your drive begins in **Patten**, which is not in Aroostook County but in Penobscot County right next door. It's a good first stop, however, because it is home to the **Patten Lumbermen's Museum,** and a visit here will give you insight into Maine's important lumber industry, a huge part of which continues to be based in Aroostook County. Nine buildings display artifacts from the life of woodsmen from the early 1800s through 1975. You'll visit an 1820 logging camp and see the specialized tools used for cutting lumber and for driving the logs along the rivers, equipment used by the camp cook, logging sleds, giant loghaulers, a blacksmith shop, and a photographic display showcasing the rugged life of the Maine lumberman.

Plan, if you can, to be here on the second Sunday in August for the museum's annual **Bean Hole Day,** when you'll be treated to a dinner much like that served by the hardworking logging camp cooks: bean-hole beans; red hot dogs (yes, they are fire-engine red and enjoyed only in Maine!); coleslaw, biscuits, boiled coffee guaranteed to keep you buzzed for hours, and homemade gingerbread. The celebration includes blacksmith and chainsaw-carving exhibitions, crafts, musical events, and activities for children. The whole thing can be quite eye-opening for traveling youngsters used to getting their entertainment electronically. The museum is located on Shin Pond Road (Route 159) just west of Route 11.

Leaving the museum on Route 11, you'll drive through long stretches of, well, not much at all. Just relax and enjoy the natural beauty you're passing through—acres and acres of thick forest, glimpses here and there of **Mount Katahdin**, eagles and hawks overhead, and if you're lucky, a moose or deer or black bear sighting. As you drive through small villages and

BAXTER STATE PARK AND MOUNT KATAHDIN

Mount Katahdin is Maine's highest peak, at 5,268 feet, and marks the northern terminus of the Appalachian Trail. The land surrounding Katahdin was a gift to Maine from former governor Percival Baxter, who purchased it with his own funds when the state declined to grant the necessary money. Today those lands, now totaling some two hundred thousand acres, are known as **Baxter State Park,** located in East Central Piscataquis County, west of Patten on Route 159. This is a state park in name only. Baxter does not receive state funds and therefore establishes its own rules, which are many, specific, and strictly enforced. Thus far those rules and regulations have been very successful in keeping Baxter in a wild and natural state that makes it especially appealing to serious hikers, intrepid backpackers, and campers. The park visitors center has a detailed handout of rules, which include no pets, motorcycles, or motorized trail bikes anywhere in the park, although you can bring in a bicycle and ride it on certain roads.

Katahdin—the name means "the greatest mountain" in the Penobscot language—is a popular destination for day climbs, with trailheads located within the park. The visitors center can suggest day hikes and inform you about climbing conditions when you arrive, but keep in mind that it's necessary to make advance reservations for some day hikes, a rule put into effect to limit overuse of certain trails. Check the website well in advance of your trip for details.

Amenities at the park are limited to rustic outhouses and a variety of camping options at ten campgrounds. Even for a short visit you should come prepared with everything you might need, including food and water (there is no drinkable water within the park) and bug repellent. Percival Baxter's legacy to the state is a glorious mountain and forested retreat that, while welcoming two-footed visitors, is first and foremost a natural wilderness home for black bears, moose, deer, and a breathtaking variety of birds and butterflies.

---

unorganized townships and plantations—designations given to Maine's most rural outposts—you'll pass a lot of seasonal camps and only a handful of amenities. Small, rustic rest areas are situated along the route, and you'll come across an occasional country store.

You'll pass through small towns like Ashland, which bills itself as "the Gateway to the North Maine Woods," and tiny **Portage** (population, about four hundred), where you can have a quiet stay at **Dean's Motor Lodge** to break up your journey. Soon you'll enter the **St. John Valley,** where the St. John River marks the border between the United States and Canada. Take a few minutes to stop at the charming town of **Eagle Lake,** where a roadside pull-off offers a beautiful view of the lake itself. A subtle change takes place as you enter the valley, with more and more signs appearing in both French and English, a legacy of the thousands of Acadians who in 1785 were forced out of Nova Scotia when they refused to pledge their allegiance to the British king. Many of their descendants are bilingual and continue to speak French at home, and you'll often hear French spoken on the street.

The Acadian exodus inspired the epic poem *Evangeline* by Henry Wadsworth Longfellow. His poem tells the tale of young sweethearts, Evangeline and Gabriel, who are separated by the "Great Upheaval," and follows Evangeline's lifelong quest to find her lover. When they are finally reunited in their old age, Gabriel dies shortly afterward in her arms. As you travel throughout the area, you'll find many monuments to their poignant love story.

Continue on to **Fort Kent**, known to winter sports enthusiasts around the country as a training center for biathletes from the United States and Canada, and for the annual **CAN-AM Crown Sled Dog Race**, which attracts mushers from Maine and nearby Canadian provinces, some of whom will go on to race in the Iditarod. The 250-mile race is the longest in the eastern United States; there are also 60-mile and 30-mile competitions. If you're in Fort Kent in winter, you'll enjoy seeing the mushers and the excited dogs showing their stuff.

The Acadian influence in the area shows up in the local cuisine, with ployes, a popular side dish, served in many restaurants. Similar to light buckwheat pancakes although always cooked on one side only, ployes are

THE BEGINNING OR THE END?

While you're in Fort Kent, be sure to check out the rustic sign that marks the beginning—or the end, depending

on which side of the sign you read and your personal point of view—of historic Route 1, which runs unbroken for 2,209 miles between Key West, Florida, and Fort Kent.

traditionally spread with butter, rolled up, and eaten with chicken stew. Today, however, ployes are often eaten much like pancakes—with maple syrup, as filled crepes, or topped with fruit as a dessert. Made in Fort Kent by the Bouchard Family Farm, ploye mix can be bought in local markets. Every August, the region celebrates this dish at the **Ploye Festival and Muskie Derby**. A giant ploye is cooked and served, and there's a ploye-eating contest, a craft fair, and other activities. Meanwhile, muskies—a type of large, freshwater fish—have their own day in the sun. The fishing derby takes place on the St. John River and its tributaries, with anglers vying for the biggest catch over the minimum 36 inches. The day ends with fireworks and street dancing.

FORT KENT BLOCKHOUSE

The only structure remaining from the bloodless Aroostook War, the two-story cedar log blockhouse in Fort Kent is entirely original. A small grove and picnic tables are tucked behind it. The blockhouse is now a National Historic Landmark.

Fort Kent has more facilities than many of the smaller towns surrounding it. If you'd like to stay overnight, the **Northern Door Inn** is centrally located. For dinner, **Swamp Buck Restaurant**, called "the Buck" by locals, has a large menu and a friendly staff. A short drive from downtown Fort Kent, on Route 161 South at Fort Kent Mills, you'll find **Doris's Café** where you'll enjoy regional cooking, including both ployes and French-Canadian poutine (french fries, cheese curds, and gravy), at its best. To get there, turn south off Route 1 onto Market Street and follow the road about 2 miles to the café. Continuing on Route 1 South, you'll have clear views of the homes and churches of New Brunswick across the pretty St. John River. You'll pass a number of active French social clubs, stores, and businesses displaying bilingual signs before arriving in **Madawaska**.

The most northeasterly town in the United States, Madawaska marks one of the country's four corners. Maine's largest cultural festival is held here each summer during the **Acadian Festival,** when the town reenacts the arrival of the Acadians in the area and puts on cultural displays and a traditional Acadian dinner. Take advantage of **Four Seasons Trail** in Madawaska to do a little walking or hiking, or mountain biking if you're so inclined. Clearly marked trails make it easy to choose one at your own ability level, and there are family options great for hiking with kids. In winter, the facility is open for cross-country skiing and snowshoeing. There's a beautiful modern lodge with tables, where you can enjoy a lunch you've brought with you (no food available on the premises). All this in an incredibly beautiful forest setting—and at no charge. Everything you see has been accomplished by volunteers with the support of the local business community—good old New England local activism at its best. To reach the lodge from Main Street in Madawaska, head up Sixth Avenue, turn right on Gerard Street, take a quick left onto Seventh Avenue, drive about 0.6 miles, and turn left on Spring Street. The lodge will be 0.2 miles on your right.

From Madawaska, continue on Route 1 through the tiny town of Grand Isle, whose population barely tops five hundred, and then into **Van Buren**. Watch for signs to the Acadian Village on the right. Here you'll find original and reproduction buildings that tell the story of the Acadians' expulsion from their homeland and the new life they created in the settlement they called Violette. (The town was later named for President Van Buren.) Among the buildings are a replica of a typical log church, an old schoolhouse, a barn, and a country store. One of the most interesting buildings is the Morneault House, a typical Acadian dwelling that gives a sense of Acadian life in the mid-19th century.

Acadians were not the only people to find Aroostook County an

The Acadian Village in Van Buren

appealing place in which to start new lives. In the summer of 1870, a group of 51 Swedish immigrants established a Swedish colony near **Caribou** that they named **New Sweden**. Over time, others would join them and develop the neighboring towns of Westmanland, Stockholm, and Woodland. In 1871 the New Sweden settlers built their first church, First Sweden Evangelical Lutheran, now the Gustof Adolph Evangelical Lutheran Church. Regular services are still held here. To reach New Sweden, travel about 16 miles from Van Buren on Route 1 and turn right on Station Road. Shortly after passing the post office, you'll find the **Lars-Noak Blacksmith Shop** and the **Larsson-Ostlund Log Home**, both of which will give you a peek into the early lives of settlers here. Both blacksmith shop and home are on the National Register of Historic Places. Beside the home is an excellent example of one of the potato barns that have long played such an important role in the economy of Aroostook County.

New Sweden remains the heart of the community, and its downtown area is the site of several original buildings. The **Capitol School**, in use until the 1950s as a school, is now a small gift shop specializing in Scandinavian items. A nearby building was once a welcoming center for new immigrants and a place for them to stay until they got settled. Burned in the 1970s and rebuilt, it's now the **New Sweden Historical Museum**. Behind the museum, the **Lindsten Stuga**, an authentic log home containing original artifacts, is occasionally opened for tours. A beautifully maintained cemetery nearby contains the graves of many early settlers.

New Sweden and the surrounding communities welcome warm weather each year with an unforgettable **Midsommar Fest**, always held around the time of the summer solstice, to which all are welcome. Even if there's not a drop of Swedish blood in you, you'll soon be caught up in the fun of making a floral headpiece adorned with lupines, daisies, and streamers, and watching the annual decorating and erecting of the maypole. Dancing follows, with many residents of New Sweden and surrounding towns dressed in traditional clothing. The celebration continues with a public supper and, the next day, with a procession carrying the maypole to Thomas Park, named for William Widgery Thomas Jr., consul to Sweden under Abraham Lincoln, who was responsible for bringing the first Swedish settlers to the area. The historic homes and buildings mentioned above are open during the Midsommar Fest; if you are here at other times of year, inquire locally about open hours.

While you're in the area, visit **Stockholm**, too, by continuing west 0.5

POTATO COUNTRY

Maine was once the country's premier potato-growing state. Although those days are gone, potatoes remain an important crop, and nowhere more so than in Aroostook County. As you drive around you'll pass field after field of potatoes, and during the fall harvest season, lots of roadside stands will be selling them, often on the honor system. It has been a long-standing tradition in Aroostook County to start school early and let children take a couple of weeks off in the fall to help bring in the potato harvest. This tradition continues, although today younger students stay in school and only teenagers are excused to work in

A rustic potato house in New Sweden, once important for long-term storage of the potato crop

the fields. Despite the hard work, many Aroostook County residents have fond memories of gaining their first experience in the working world in the cool air of a northern Maine autumn. Beside the fields, you'll see old and new examples of potato barns—locally known as potato houses—where the crop is temporarily stored. The older, rustic potato barns along Route 164 make for great photo opportunities.

mile on Station Road and turning right onto Route 161. After 5 miles, turn right onto Stockholm Road. There's a wonderful little general store here called **Anderson's**, in business since 1906. You can buy basic necessities at Anderson's and even have a breakfast of strong coffee and pastries at a table you'll probably share with a local or two. Nearby, restored **Eureka Hall** is a great stop for a down-home dinner with Swedish flair—or for very un-Swedish pizza.

When you're ready, return to Route 161 and follow it south into Caribou, home of Susan Collins, one of Maine's two women senators. The **Caribou Inn & Convention Center** makes a good stopping point at the end of a long day of driving. The friendly bar is popular with locals heading home from work or out for the evening on the weekend, and there's a small restaurant as well if you don't feel like going out for a meal.

LET IT SNOW...AND SNOW!
Aroostook County averages about 115 inches of snow a year, making it popular for all kinds of winter sports, including snowmobiling along twenty-three hundred miles of trails. Snow is pretty much guaranteed by December, and continues through March and often into April.

Among Caribou's attractions is the **Nylander Museum,** housing the collections of Olof Nylander, a Swedish naturalist. After moving to the United States, Nylander became interested in the natural history of Maine and amassed a huge collection of rocks, shells, and Native American artifacts, among many other items, most of which he documented and wrote about in detail. It's an intriguing stop for anyone interested in science.

From Caribou, drive along scenic Route 164, where you will find eye-catching photo opportunities around every curve. You'll pass acres and acres of potato fields interspersed with green meadows, white farmhouses, and old and new potato barns, all under a canopy of blue skies and white clouds. If you happen to be passing through **Washburn** on the third weekend in August, stop by the annual August Festival, a true down-home event taking place on Main Street. You'll feel as if you've stepped back to a simpler time as you enjoy a parade and wander around booths selling chicken barbecue and other food, maple syrup, and crafts. The 1852 **Benjamin Wilder Home** and nearby **Aroostook Agricultural Museum** will be open, an example of a mid-19th-century farmstead plus a rustic country museum filled with wooden tools, sleighs, early make-you-cringe dental equipment, pottery, and other relics of everyday life from long ago. Even if you

Well-used hand tools in the Aroostook Agricultural Museum

miss the festival, be sure to hop up on a stool in the iconic **Washburn Coffee Shop** on Main Street and watch the world go by. You'll soon be chatted up by a local, curious to know what has brought you to this laid-back little town of about sixteen hundred people.

Continuing on Route 164, head south on Route 1 to **Presque Isle**, starting point for the largest three-dimensional scale model (scale is 1:93,000,000) of the solar system in the world. The **Maine Solar System Model**, built as a community project, begins with a 50-foot diameter sun located on the campus of the University of Maine at Presque Isle and ends 40 miles later with a teeny Pluto in **Houlton.** Along the way, most other planets are perched on poles for easy viewing from the car.

When you get to Houlton, stop for a bite to eat downtown at **Zippy's**, a local fast-food-with-flare institution, before continuing on to **Oakfield** on I-95, the final stop on your tour. Railroad buffs will want to stop here

Among the attractions at the Oakfield Railroad Museum are a caboose and a miniature of the railroad station.

to visit the **Oakfield Railroad Museum**, an homage to the old Bangor & Aroostook Railroad that features an authentic wooden station, various railroad cars including a caboose that's lots of fun for children to explore, signal lanterns, telegraph equipment, and centuries-old photos. The volunteer docents, many of them former railroad employees, are enthusiastic and knowledgeable. It's a bit tricky to reach the museum: From I-95 South, take Exit 286 and turn left onto Oakfield-Smyrna Street. Turn left onto Main Street, cross the bridge, and turn right onto Station Street and go to the end, where you'll find the museum.

If you'd like to spend the night before ending your tour, you'll get a warm welcome from Gina Clarke at **Yellow House B&B**, where cookies on your arrival and a big country breakfast in the morning will make you feel like a pampered guest in a friend's home.

Like most visitors to the County, you'll probably be reluctant to tear yourself away, but when it's time to end your journey, just return to I-95 South to head back to your starting point in Portland.

IN THE AREA

Accommodations

Caribou Inn & Convention Center, 19 Main Street, Caribou. Phone: 207-498-3733; www.caribouinn.com. Inexpensive.

Dean's Motor Lodge, 2075 Portage Lake Road, Portage. Phone: 207-435-3701; www.deansmotorlodge.com. Restaurant and lounge on the premises. Inexpensive.

Northern Door Inn, 356 West Main Street, Fort Kent. Phone: 1-866-834-3133; www.northerndoorinn.com. Inexpensive; includes continental breakfast.

Yellow House Bed & Breakfast, 270 Ridge Road, Oakfield. Phone: 1-888-261-8808; www.yellowhousebedandbreakfast.com. Inexpensive; includes full breakfast.

Dining

Doris's Café, 345 Market Street, Fort Kent Mills. Phone: 207-834-6262. Down-home local cooking makes this a winner. Inexpensive.

Eureka Hall, 5 School Street, Stockholm. Phone: 207-896-3196. Open Thurs.–Sat. for dinner and for brunch on Sun. Inexpensive.

Swamp Buck Restaurant, 250 West Main Street, Fort Kent. Phone: 207-834-3055. Inexpensive to moderate.

Washburn Coffee Shop, Main Street, Washburn. Open 5 AM–2:30 PM. Very inexpensive.

Zippy's, 20 Market Square, Houlton. Phone: 207-532-5678. A few tables for outside dining plus takeout service. A big menu and surprisingly tasty fast food. Open spring through early fall. Very inexpensive.

Attractions and Recreation

Acadian Festival, Madawaska. Phone: 207-728-6250; www.acadian festival.com. Held each summer; call or check website for dates.

Acadian Village, Route 1, Van Buren. Phone; 207-868-5042; www
.connectmaine.com/acadianvillage. From June 15–Sept. 15, open daily,
12–5. Admission: Adults, $6; students, $3.

Baxter State Park and Mount Katahdin. Phone: 207-723-5140; www
.baxterstateparkauthority.com. Enter the park at Togue Point Gate about
18 miles east of Millinocket or at Matagamon Gate in the park's northeast
corner. Gates are open dawn to dusk from spring through fall; see website
for details and for winter information. Maine residents admitted free of
charge for day use; $14 fee for nonresidents.

Benjamin Wilder Home and **Aroostook Agricultural Museum,** 17
Main Street, Washburn. Much of Washburn's annual August Festival takes
place in front of these two buildings. Phone: 207-455-4339; www.pi
chamber.com/demographics-mainmenu-29/washburn-mainmenu-95
.html.

CAN-AM Crown Sled Dog Race, Fort Kent. Phone: 207-444-5439;
http://can-am.sjv.net. The race starts and finishes in downtown Fort
Kent. See website for dates and details of other spectator points. For obvious reasons, spectators are asked not to bring their own dogs near the
race. No fee for spectators.

Fort Kent Blockhouse, off Route 1 (watch for signs), Ft. Kent. Phone:
207-941-4014. You can walk around the outside of the blockhouse when-
ever weather makes it accessible; call for open hours. No fee.

Four Seasons Trail, Spring Street, Madawaska. Contact: www.four
seasonstrail.org. Facility is open year-round and visitors are warmly welcomed. No charge, but this is a volunteer operation and donations are
gratefully accepted.

Lars-Noak Blacksmith Shop, Larsson-Ostland Log Home, and other
historic buildings in New Sweden. For information: www.aroostook.me
.us/newsweden.

Maine Solar System Scale Model, Route 1 between Presque Isle and
Houlton. For information: www.umpi.maine.edu/info/nmms/solar. Free.

Midsommar Fest, New Sweden. Phone: 207-896-5240; www.maine
swedishcolony.info.

Nylander Museum, 657 Main Street, Caribou. Phone: 207-493-4209. Open from Memorial Day through Labor Day, Fri. and Sat., 9–5, and by appointment. Winter hours by appointment only.

Oakfield Railroad Museum, Station Street, Oakfield. Phone: 207-757-8575; www.oakfieldmuseum.org. Open from Sat. before Memorial Day through Labor Day, Sat.–Sun., 1–4. Free; donations appreciated.

Patten Lumberman's Museum, Shin Pond Road (Route 159), Patten. Phone: 207-528-2650; www.lumbermensmuseum.org. Open from Memorial Day weekend through June 30, Fri.–Sun., 10–4. From July 1 through Columbus Day weekend, open Tues.–Sun., 10–4. Also open all Mon. holidays from spring through fall. Adults: $8; seniors, $7; children 6–11, $3; under 6, no charge.

Ploye Festival and Muskie Derby, Fort Kent. Ploye Festival information: Phone: 207-834-5354; www.fortkentchamber.com. Muskie Derby information: Phone: 207-834-3507; www.fortkent-muskie.com. Held the second weekend in August. See website for exact dates and activities.

Shopping

Anderson's Store, 327 North Main Street, Stockholm. Phone: 207-896-5858. There must be something you need to buy, even if it's just a coffee or the local newspaper. Don't miss this friendly place!

Capitol School and Gift Shop, New Sweden. Contact: aroostook.me .us/newsweden. Summer hours are usually Wed.–Sun., 12–4.

Other Contacts

Aroostook County Information: www.visitaroostook.com.

Information on Maine's Native American peoples and their languages: www.native-languages.org/maine.htm.

Smalls Falls tumbles into a clear pool in Madrid.

CHAPTER

13

Maine: The Rangeley Lakes Region

Estimated length: About 125 miles from Portland to Oquossuc; 110 miles to tour the area.

Estimated time: Allow 3 hours driving time from Portland. You'll need a weekend to thoroughly explore Rangeley and environs.

Getting there: Leaving Portland, take Forest Avenue heading north, which becomes Route 302 after a few miles. After about 30 miles, turn right onto Route 35 toward Harrison and on to Bethel. Take Route 2 North to Mexico, then turn left onto Route 17 North to Oquossuc.

Highlights: Fishing. Hunting. Hiking, biking, boating, and birding. Swimming, skating, skiing, and wildlife watching. In short, if you love to be out-of-doors, Rangeley has just about everything, including the opportunity to canoe the pristine **Northern Forest Canoe Trail** and enjoy fabulous scenic views like that at the **Height of Land Overlook**. Add some excellent museums, like the **Rangeley Outdoor Sporting Heritage Museum;** shops selling made-in-Maine products; and cozy inns and restaurants, and you have a weekend drive that can't be beat. Come at any time of year depending on your interests. There's great winter skiing, spring and summer are glorious for fishing and swimming in the Rangeley Lakes Region's 111 lakes and ponds, and fall brings cool days for hiking, along with magnificent foliage. This is one of the country's few remaining pristine vacation spots, where you can truly get as far away from it all as you wish.

Four thousand years before the first Europeans recognized the beauty and bounty of the area now known as the Rangeley Lakes Region, Native Americans had set up hunting and fishing camps where they spent much of their time between the spring ice-out and the first snowfall of winter. The Abenaki made good use of the plentiful birch trees, still much in evidence around Rangeley, to build birch bark-covered wigwams and the light but strong canoes for which they became well known, and used other trees, including spruce and balsam, for food and medicine. Native Americans employed the connecting waterways of Maine, New Hampshire, Vermont, New York, and Quebec as a sort of highway, and serious paddlers can still canoe all or part of the 740-mile route along the **Northern Forest Canoe Trail.**

In the mid-18th-century, white explorers began to take note of the area's abundant wildlife and other natural resources, but it was not until 1825 and the arrival of James Rangeley that a permanent white settlement was founded. Rangeley established himself as landlord over an estate farmed by several tenants. Known in the English tradition as Squire Rangeley, he seems to have been widely respected, helped build the area's first sawmill and gristmill, and 15 years later left behind a thriving settlement when he moved from the area following the tragic death of a daughter.

Farming and logging were the lifeblood of Rangeley in its earliest days. A long history of transporting logs by log drives along Maine's waterways ended in the 1970s; today you'll pass enormous trucks carrying harvested timber to market. It was fishing, however, that first brought national attention to Rangeley. "Sports," or outdoorsmen "from away"—mostly from New York, Boston, and other Eastern cities—began coming to Rangeley by narrow-gauge railroad and steamboat around 1860, lured by tales of brook trout weighing as much as 11 pounds. Families soon followed, beginning a tradition of vacationing in grand hotels and inns for the summer season. The tradition of staying in one place for the entire summer waned after World War II, but fishermen continued to arrive and try their luck at catching an elusive brookie or landlocked salmon. Today their vacations may be shorter, but families still flock to Rangeley to take advantage of its natural beauty and wide range of outdoor activities. And for fishermen, Rangeley remains a special place.

You'll realize that tales of the Rangeley area's extraordinary scenery

The view from the Height of Land Overlook in Oquossoc

are not exaggerated when you arrive at the **Height of Land Overlook** on Route 17 in **Oquossoc.** At some point in your visit, try to come here at dusk and bring your camera. You'll never forget the sight of the sun setting in a blaze of scarlet, pink, and gold over Mooselookmeguntic Lake and New Hampshire's White Mountains in the distance. Chances are, your first view of the overlook will be by day with clouds drifting overhead and sunlight dappling the water, a memorable sight in itself. When you can tear yourself away, continue on to the **Rangeley Outdoor Sporting Heritage Museum**, dedicated to preserving the stories of the hunters and fishermen of yesteryear. Included in the collection are more than 150 flies designed and tied by the famous Carrie Stevens (1882–1970), whose Gray Ghost fly is legendary among serious anglers. Also of interest are mounted trout and salmon by Herb Welch, perhaps the best taxidermist of his day, along with many of his paintings.

Be sure to check out the authentic 1890s sporting camp that has been dismantled and then reassembled inside the museum. A handsome birch bark table and a set of trophy moose antlers with a spread of 61 inches decorate the interior.

Carrie Stevens was not the only local woman to find a place in the history of fly-fishing. Advised by a doctor to get plenty of fresh air to improve her health, Cornelia Crosby (1854-1946), born in nearby Phillips, Maine, began hunting and fishing in the Rangeley area and soon christened herself

"Fly Rod Crosby." Her expertise with a fly rod became the stuff of legend as she guided lesser anglers to the best fishing spots. When Maine began registering Maine Guides, Fly Rod received license number 1 in recognition of her expertise and all she had done to promote the state as a prime vacation spot. She stood six feet tall, and photos show her fishing and shooting in a hat and a dress with a fitted bodice, long puffy sleeves, and a skirt that swept the ground—all appropriate attire for a woman of that era. When she was in her forties and hired to travel around the country to extol the attractions of Maine in general and Rangeley in particular, she showed up at the 1898 Sportsman's Exposition in New York City in a skirt widely reported to be a scandalous 8 inches off the floor. By all accounts, Fly Rod's ankles brought as much attention to Rangeley's diverse beauty as did the stuffed trout and other exhibits she brought along to illustrate her lectures. Before she died at age 92, apparently having benefited quite nicely from her doctor's prescription of fresh air and sunshine, Fly Rod was often quoted as saying, "I would rather fish any day than go to heaven."

Time to try your own luck in the woods? **River's Edge Sports** in Oquossoc can set you up with a fishing or hunting license, bait, canoe or kayak rentals, fly-fishing lessons, and even a fishing guide. With several area lakes—Rangeley, Mooselookmeguntic, Cupsuptic, Upper and Lower Richardson, Kennebago, and Umbagog among them—to choose from, your only problem will be which one to try first. For nonfishermen who want to get out on the water, River's Edge Sports offers a terrific self-guided

Sign on display at the Rangeley Outdoor Sporting Heritage Museum

canoe trip on the Kennebago River. You'll canoe at your own pace through mostly very calm waters, ending near your car. The trip normally takes two or three hours, after which River's Edge Sports will pick up the canoe and you can be on your way.

At some point while you are in Oquossoc, enjoy a meal at the charming **Gingerbread House**. One part of the building has been a market and an ice cream shop in its previous lives, and a nostalgic 1950s ice cream fountain is still on the premises. You can drop in after dinner for dessert or just come in for an afternoon snack. But don't miss having a meal here, too. Austrian-trained chef Dean Szablewski knows his way around a kitchen, there's a decent wine list, and the waitstaff is cheery and competent. All in all, this is an unexpected find tucked away on the corner of Routes 4 and 17.

If you'd prefer to sit back and relax rather than paddle, you can take a cruise on the *Oquossoc Lady* on Rangeley, Mooselookmeguntic, or Cupsuptic lakes, enjoy the spectacular scenery, and learn a little about the history of the Rangeley region.

At some point you'll probably want to experience Rangeley on your own two feet. Whether you're a novice hiker or an experienced backpacker,

---

ABOUT THOSE LAKE NAMES

The Abenaki named many of the lakes in this part of Maine, defining each lake by its most notable characteristic. Among them are the tongue-twisting Mooselookmeguntic ("place where the moose come to feed"), Cupsuptic ("closed-up water"—probably so named because it is narrow and surrounded by a thick stand of trees), Umbagog ("shallow lake"), and Kennebago ("sweet flowing water").

---

you'll find a wealth of hiking trails around Rangeley. Before starting out, be sure you have the necessary gear and clothing to deal with Maine's erratic weather, and plenty of food and water. Let someone know your plans and when you expect to return. Do your part to keep the area pristine by staying on marked trails and carrying out everything you carry in. Three of the most popular hikes are those to **Smalls Falls, Saddleback Mountain,** and **Piazza Rock.** Smalls Falls is located 12 miles south of Rangeley on Route 4. Scenic and easily hiked, with picnic tables readily available, the trail winds along a stream and leads to other falls. Bring your bathing suit along, because you can swim here or just wade in the cold, clear water. If you're more adventurous—and skilled—you can hike to the summit of 4,120-ft. Saddleback Mountain from the base lodge at **Saddleback Resort,** following one of several routes to the top. Be sure to have warm and waterproof clothing on hand for this hike, as weather at the top may be quite different from what you start out in. To take the Piazza Rock hike, an easy 2.8-mile round trip that ends at an interesting rock formation, drive 9 miles south of Rangeley and enter the Appalachian Trail where it crosses Route 4. The Appalachian Trail extends across the summit of Saddleback Mountain. Complete information on these and other hiking trails is available from the **Rangeley Lakes Area Chamber of Commerce** on Park Street, just off Main Street.

At this point you may be ready to check into a bed & breakfast or hotel. In Rangeley, try the **Pleasant Street Inn Bed & Breakfast,** on a quiet street just a short walk from the downtown shops and restaurants. Owners Rob and Jan Welch (she is a lifelong Mainer and former nationally ranked skier) will not only feed you a hearty country breakfast but are also adept at planning drives, hikes, and fishing or canoeing trips or pointing out the best spots for leaf peeping or moose watching. There are excellent eateries in Rangeley as well, including the elegant but unpretentious **Loon Lodge Inn and Restaurant,** where dinner in the main restaurant or the casual Pickford Pub is often capped off with a glorious sunset over Rangeley Lake.

If seeing a moose is on your agenda, the area around Rangeley is prime territory. A great way to see them while taking a break from your own driving is on **Saddleback Moose Tours**' pickle bus (guess what color it is), which leaves from the Saddleback Guest Service Center in downtown Rangeley.

Downtown Rangeley has a number of little shops and restaurants. The **Alpine Shop** sells Maine-made items and necessities for hiking and camping. **Ecopelagicon** has a variety of nature items, and you can rent a canoe or kayak here for a leisurely paddle around Haley Pond right out back. For an unrushed meal or a glass of wine and an appetizer, or for flaky homemade croissants in the heart of the Maine woods, try **Corner Side** in a beautifully decorated location right on Main Street.

Several interesting driving loops begin and end at or near Rangeley—pick up a list at the chamber of commerce and choose one that looks appealing. These routes are especially good in fall when the leaves change. Keep in mind that these routes wind through small villages with charming scenery but few services.

A typical drive is the **Franklin Heritage Loop**. Begin by heading east on Route 16 toward Stratton, stopping for a visit to the **Rangeley Logging Museum** with its displays of logging equipment, saws, sleds, a bateau (a slim boat used in the log drives), chainsaw carvings, and period photos. A series

Main Street, Rangeley

of paintings by Alden Grant provides a look at daily life in an early logging camp. The museum hosts a logging festival on the fourth Saturday in July, complete with a parade of logging trucks and a bean-hole supper.

Leaving the museum, continue through Rangeley to Stratton (the local "Moose Alley"), then head south on Route 27 and through Carrabassett Valley, where you might stop for a meal at lively little **Hugs,** a local favorite specializing in Italian food. Then travel on to **Kingfield** and into **New Portland**, following the signs to the intriguing **Wire Bridge,** an engineering marvel built in 1866 of cable brought from England. You can drive across the bridge, which spans the Carrabassett River, but be prepared to shake, rattle, and roll as you undulate your way across. This is the oldest suspension bridge in Maine and is thought to be the only one of its type in the country.

Also in New Portland, you'll find **Nowetah's American Indian Museum and Store,** a shop featuring jewelry, crafts, and baskets made by the Abenaki as well as members of other tribes from across the United States, Canada, and South America. You can shop for inexpensive trinkets or incredibly detailed woven baskets and beaded headdresses. The small museum displays some handsome vintage items not for sale. Nowetah her-

MOOSE WATCHING

"God created all the animals, then used the spare parts to make the moose," say old-timers in rural Maine. Nearsighted, with lugubrious faces, ungainly bodies, and skinny legs, moose are indeed unusual-looking creatures. Traveling in the Rangeley area from spring through early winter, chances are you'll see one or more moose, especially along the stretch of Route 16 extending from Rangeley to Stratton. Prime time for a successful moose watch here is in the early morning or at dusk from late spring to midsummer and again during the month of September.

Vegetarians consuming 40 to 50 pounds of food a day, moose are born in the early spring weighing 20 to 35 pounds, grow to their full size within a couple of years, and reach maturity around age five. Many live to age twenty. A full-grown male—called a bull—can measure 10 feet long, 7 feet at the shoulders, with long, skinny legs, and may weigh twelve hundred pounds or more. Females, or cows, weigh up to nine hundred pounds. The bull's rack can have a span of more than 60 inches. Shed over the winter, moose racks are a popular tourist souvenir. The statewide moose population is estimated at around thirty thousand, surpassed in number only by the moose herds in Alaska. Licenses for Maine's annual hunt are distributed in a very competitive lottery.

Each year, collisions—some fatal to both moose and car occupants—are reported, so drive with caution, especially in areas marked with a moose sign and blinking lights, an indication that there are moose nearby.

Usually quite docile animals, bulls can be aggressive during the rutting season from mid-September through mid-October, as are cows with calves in tow in spring and summer. Awkward looking they may be, but a provoked moose can travel up to 35 miles an hour. Obviously it's not a wise idea to annoy a twelve-hundred-pound animal, so when you spot a moose, keep a respectful distance or watch and photograph it from the safety of your parked car.

---

self is a fountain of knowledge about local Native American history and crafts.

From New Portland, continue south on Route 27. At New Vineyard, turn right on Route 234 toward Strong, then take Route 4 North toward Phillips. **Hunnisett Reed English Antiques** is located on Main Street in tiny Phillips, and you can even have a proper British afternoon tea in the midst of all the treasures. From Phillips, the Franklin Heritage Loop continues on through Madrid, where if you haven't had a chance to see **Smalls Falls**

The unusual Wire Bridge in New Portland

earlier, you might do so now. Even for nonhikers, it's an easy walk to the first set of falls. From here the loop brings you right back to Rangeley on Route 4, ending a pleasant day trip. You might want to review the day over a pizza at **The Red Onion**, a fixture on Main Street for more than 40 years where locals will be glad to fill you in on their favorite hikes and fishing spots. And if you're not quite ready for your journey to end, the **Rangeley Saddleback Inn** is just a few minutes away.

If you've wisely dispensed with your cell phone, laptop, and other electronic gear during this trip, you may find yourself less than enthusiastic about heading back to a busy, high-tech life. But Rangeley will be here when you return someday, probably looking much the same then as it does now and as it did 50 years ago. No one's in a great hurry for things to change, and after your first visit, you won't be either. When you do have to leave it all behind, first head west for 7 miles on Route 4 into Oquossoc. Then turn left onto Route 17 and return to Portland.

THE STANLEY STEAMER STORY

If you'd like to take a break from your travels as you explore the Franklin Heritage Loop, you can stay at a longtime Rangeley-area favorite, the **Herbert Hotel** in Kingfield, and check out an intriguing little museum in the same town.

Kingfield was the home of F.E. and F.O. Stanley, identical-twin brothers who designed and built the Stanley steam car. Several cars are on display at the **Stanley Museum**, housed in the former Stanley School, which was designed and funded by the brothers in 1903 as a gift for their hometown. When the building

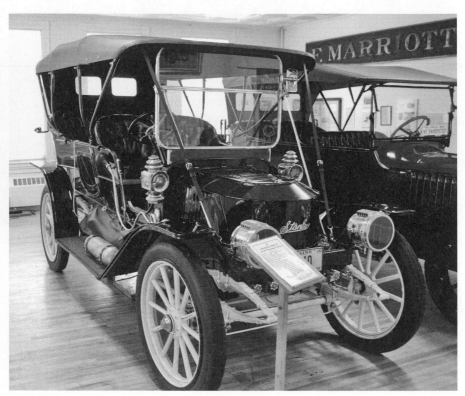

A 1910 Stanley Steamer at Kingfield's Stanley Museum

became obsolete and faced razing, it was taken over by the museum to house Stanley steamers, family archives, photography by the twins' talented sister, Chansonetta, and other memorabilia. Car buffs will be enthralled, and everyone will be intrigued by the winsome photographs and such items as a 19-point checklist for cranking up a Stanley steamer that includes an admonition to "Have a fire extinguisher nearby."

IN THE AREA

Accommodations

Herbert Hotel, 246 Maine Street (Route 27), Kingfield. Phone: 207-265-2000; www.herbertgrandhotel.com. Seasonal packages available. Very inexpensive.

Loon Lodge Inn and Restaurant, 16 Pickford Road, Rangeley. Phone: 207-864-5666; www.loonlodgeme.com. Comfortable rooms with beautiful views and a lakeside lawn that's perfect for an evening stroll or to let the kids run off some steam. Inquire about packages. Inexpensive to moderate.

Pleasant Street Inn and B&B, 104 Pleasant Street, Rangeley. Phone: 207-864-5916; www.pleasantstreetinnbb.com. Spotlessly clean with lovely quilts on the beds and charming hosts who will help you make the most of your Rangeley visit; close to town. Inexpensive to moderate; includes full breakfast.

Rangeley Saddleback Inn, 2303 Main Street, Rangeley. Phone: 207-864-3434. Some rooms overlook Rangeley Lake; some are pet friendly. Small pub on the premises. Snowmobile trail in back makes this a good choice for winter travelers. Inexpensive.

Dining

Corner Side, 2485 Main Street, Rangeley. Phone: 207-864-2883; www.atthecornerside.com. A bistro-like atmosphere with a cheerful waitstaff and excellent food—the raspberry croissants, creative salads, and seafood soups and entrées are outstanding. Open for breakfast, lunch, and dinner. Moderate.

Gingerbread House, Route 4 (at the corner of Routes 4 and 17), Oquossoc. Phone: 207-864-3602; www.gingerbreadhouserestaurant.net. Friendly and fun, and popular with the locals, which is always a good sign. A variety of entrées and a nice list of wines by the glass or bottle. Open for breakfast, lunch, and dinner. Moderate.

Hugs, 3001 Town Line Road (Route 27), Carrabassett. Phone: 207-237-2392. Specializes in northern Italian dishes. Informal; popular with skiers. Moderate.

Loon Lodge Inn and Restaurant, 16 Pickford Road, Rangeley. Phone: 207-864-5666; www.loonlodgeme.com. Good food and friendly service make this a winner. Open for lunch and dinner. Moderate to expensive in main restaurant; inexpensive to moderate in the pub.

The Red Onion, Main Street, Rangeley. Phone: 207-864-5022; www .rangeleyredonion.com. Home-style meals, including vegetarian choices, as well as pizza. Very family-friendly. Inexpensive.

Attractions and Recreation

Oquossoc Lady, Oquossoc. Phone: 207-864-2038; www.rangeleylake cruises.com. Rates vary with cruise chosen; call or check website for details.

Rangeley Logging Museum, Route 16 East, Rangeley. Phone: 207-864-3939; www.mason.gmu.edu/~myocom/yocomroad/maine/logging _museum/main_rlrlm.html. Open weekends in July and Aug., 11–2, and by appointment. Donations and new memberships welcomed.

Rangeley Outdoor Sporting Heritage Museum, Route 4, Oquossoc. Phone: 207-864-3091; www.rangeleyoutdoormuseum.org. Check website or call for open hours at the time of your visit.

Saddleback Mountain Resort, Dallas Hill Road off Route 4, Rangeley. Phone: 207-864-5671; www.saddlebackmaine.com. Alpine and cross-country skiing in winter; hiking, moose watching, and music events in other seasons. A small snack bar is open daily except Sun. for light lunches and snacks convenient to take along while hiking. See website for lift prices and announcements of other events.

Saddleback Moose Tours, Saddleback Guest Service Center, 2473 Main Street, Rangeley. Phone: 207-864-5496; www.saddlebackmaine.com. Hour-long moose-watching tours depart around dusk on Tues. and Thurs. during the warm-weather months. Free; advance reservations required.

Stanley Museum, 40 School Street, Kingfield. Phone: 207-265-2729; www.stanleymuseum.org. Call for open hours. Small admission fee.

Shopping

Alpine Shop, 2504 Main Street, Rangeley. Phone: 207-864-3741. Sells clothing, including rugged hiking and camping clothes and boots, and a variety of souvenir items for adults and kids. Open daily.

Ecopelagicon, 7 Pond Street, Rangeley. Phone: 207-864-2771; www .ecopelagicon.com. Wonderful nature books, CDs, maps, and other goodies, plus canoes and kayaks to rent by the hour or day. Open daily from Memorial Day to Columbus Day; call for open days and times during the winter season.

Hunnisett Reed English Antiques, 53 Main Street, Phillips. Phone: 207-639-2952. English country furniture, pottery and porcelain, linens, tea-related collectibles, and more. Serves a charming British high tea in the afternoon. Open Tues.–Sat., 10–4.

Nowetah's American Indian Museum and Store, 2 Colegrove Road (Route 27), New Portland. Phone: 207-628-4981; www.nowetahs.webs .com. Crafts and gifts in the store; free admission to the small museum. Open daily throughout the year.

Other Contacts

Northern Forest Canoe Trail, PO Box 565, Waitsfield, Vermont. Phone: 802-496-2285; www.northernforestcanoetrail.org. Provides maps and information for paddling the ancient routes taken by Native Americans, including those through the Rangeley lakes.

River's Edge Sports, Route 4, Oquossoc. Phone: 207-864-5582; www .riversedgesports.com. Canoe, kayak, and snowmobile rentals; hunting and fishing licenses; guided lake trips; clothing and gear. Open year-round.

Rangeley Lakes Region Chamber of Commerce, 6 Park Road (off Main Street), Rangeley. Phone: 207-864-5364; www.rangeleymaine.com.

NORWAY 14 MI.
PARIS 15 MI.
DENMARK 23 MI.
NAPLES 23 MI.
SWEDEN 25 MI.
POLAND 27 MI.
MEXICO 37 MI.
PERU 46 MI.
CHINA 94 MI.

A sign points the way to internationally named towns in Maine.

CHAPTER

14

Maine: The Sebago Lake Region

Estimated length: About 17 miles from Portland to Gray; about 135 miles to drive the route.

Estimated time: Allow about 30 minutes from Portland. Although you can drive it in a day, this trip makes a nice weekend excursion, especially if you'd like to spend time on the water or at a festival or fair.

Getting there: From Portland take I-95 (the Maine Turnpike) North to Exit 63 to Gray. Then take Route 26 North four miles to the Maine Wildlife Park on the right, where your tour begins.

Highlights: Not far from Portland, yet miles away from the hustle-bustle of city life, the timeless communities of western Maine are situated against a backdrop of rolling mountains and crystal-clear lakes. Swimming, boating, and fishing are the order of the day. Along the way you'll visit sites as diverse as the **Maine Wildlife Park,** dedicated to injured animals, the last active Shaker community in the United States at **Sabbathday Lake Shaker Village**, and an old-fashioned harvest fair. Take in a blues festival, stay at one of Maine's popular resorts, where generations of the same families return year after year, participate in all the goings-on, including a ride on the *Songo Queen II* at Maine's second-largest lake, or just kick back in a deck chair and take it easy.

Enjoying a family picnic at the Maine Wildlife Park

The rockbound coast and pounding ocean surf spell *Maine* to many visitors, but beautiful as the coastal areas are, you won't want to miss this very different part of Maine, with its spellbinding lakes and abundant wildlife. For a quick peek at Maine's diverse wild creatures, start your tour with a visit to the **Maine Wildlife Park** in Gray, where orphaned or abandoned animals—or those raised in captivity and no longer able to fend for themselves in the wild—find permanent homes. Housed in natural enclosures are animals ranging from black bears to barred owls, moose, coyotes, and dozens more. The park's purpose is education, so there is always something going on here. On Saturdays, especially, you might learn about the molting habits of lobsters or the family lives of wolves, practice fly tying or fly casting, attend a lecture on raptors, or take in a concert. The park is a convenient place to stop for a picnic on a hot summer day, and if you have children along, you'll find it to be an especially good spot for them to stretch their legs as they walk around visiting the animals. You'll need to bring your own lunch, but ample picnic tables are scattered among the shade trees. Be sure to have a few quarters on hand to buy feed for the animals.

For a very different experience, when you leave the park turn right on Route 26 and drive about 4 miles to visit tranquil **Sabbathday Lake Shak-**

er Village, the only remaining active Shaker community in the country. The history of this religion is a long and fascinating one, beginning with the Quakers of England, from whom the Shakers, who preferred a more emotional and intense form of worship, splintered off in 1747. Their worship often included a whirling and twirling form of ecstatic dancing, which gave them the name "Shaking Quakers" and, eventually, "Shakers." Harassed for their beliefs in England, eight Shakers and their leader, Ann Lee ("Mother Ann"), came to the United States in 1774. By 1780 believers were persecuted here as well. Nonetheless, and despite the sect's requirement that all members pool their worldly goods, embrace pacifism, and take a vow of celibacy, the Shakers prospered and eventually established 18 communities, including several in Maine.

Celibacy meant that no followers were being born into the community, so Sabbathday Lake, like other Shaker villages, built its congregation through adult conversions. A number of widows and widowers, especially those left alone with children, joined the group, welcoming the help of the Shaker Brothers and Sisters in raising their families. In addition, for many years the village took in orphans and raised them communally, a practice that ended when adoption laws changed.

Sabbathday Lake, one of the smallest Shaker villages, was founded in 1783 and had fewer than two hundred members at its peak. Today there are three. The property, with its dwelling buildings and meetinghouse situated on eighteen hundred acres of prime farmland, is a National Historic Landmark. Visitors are welcome at Sunday services in the meetinghouse and can explore other buildings on the property on guided tours. The work of the farm, including maintenance of the grounds and gardens and caring for a flock of sheep, a herd of cows, and assorted domestic animals, is carried out by the world's three remaining Shakers, a few paid staff, and a number of volunteers. Should the sect die out, which seems inevitable at this point, agreements have been made with nonprofit agencies to maintain the land for agricultural purposes; as with other Shaker communities, the village itself will probably become a museum.

A shop on the grounds sells Shaker products including the herbs and herbal teas the community has sold for more than two hundred years. Before you leave, pay a visit to the poignant graveyard, where all the believers' graves are marked by a single gravestone reading "Shakers." "'Tis a gift to be simple," says an old Shaker hymn, and as you depart this peaceful village, you may feel that they were on to something.

From the Shaker village, continue north on Route 26 for about 9 miles and turn left on Route 11. After about 13 miles, Route 11 becomes Routes 11/35/302; continue for 2 miles to the center of **Naples**. If you'd like to base yourself in Naples for an overnight stay, the popular **Augustus Bove House** is easy to find at the corner of Routes 302 and 114. Naples is home to the *Songo River Queen II,* and while it may seem a tad surreal to see a Mississippi River stern paddle wheeler (OK, a reproduction thereof) afloat on a lake in Maine, the *Songo River Queen II* has been around since 1982, providing rides on Long Lake and the Songo River. You can't miss it; it's tied up at the Causeway just beyond the swing bridge, which opens every two hours from 8 AM to 8 PM during the summer season. The Causeway is the bustling center of everything in Naples.

SHAKER INVENTIONS

Although they live a simple, peaceful life, Shakers have always been known for their skill in creating beautiful furniture and for their technological expertise. Among their inventions at the various villages were the flat broom, the apple peeler, the washing machine, the circular saw, and the clothespin. Examples of these and other Shaker inventions are on display at Sabbathday Lake.

Aboard the *Songo River Queen II,* you can spend a pleasant hour or two on the water and learn a bit about the history of the area while enjoying the scenery. The Songo River has long been considered one of the cleanest and prettiest in North America, and in the days when steam-powered craft plied the waters, New England poets like Ralph Waldo Emerson, Nathaniel Hawthorne, and Henry Wadsworth Longfellow frequently came aboard the steamships to enjoy the picturesque surroundings and views of the White Mountains. A cruise can be a relaxing break in your travels and, if you're here in the autumn, a great way to see fall foliage while avoiding heavy traffic. Of course, if you'd rather explore the lake by piloting a boat yourself, that's possible, too. The nearby **Causeway Marina** will be happy to rent you one.

If you opt to cruise aboard the *Songo River Queen II,* try to get on a trip that passes through the hand-operated Songo Lock in **Sebago Lake State Park**. The lock connects Sebago Lake and Long Lake, allowing boaters to pass between the two bodies of water. The Songo Lock is the only one remaining of the 27 once in operation along the Cumberland and Oxford Canal, which was constructed over several years and opened in 1832 to connect Portland with Sebago Lake. It's the only lock left in the United

The Songo River Queen II *in Naples*

States today. In the canal's heyday, a fleet of boats, each about 60 feet long, transported freight and passengers. The canal's use diminished as travelers turned more to train and car travel and much of it was abandoned. The Songo Lock is still in use by pleasure boats, an interesting footnote to the days when the nation's waterways played an important role in moving both goods and people.

Naples is a lighthearted, happy place that gets the blues every June. Each year, on Father's Day weekend, the town hosts the popular **Maine Blues Festival,** welcoming blues bands from all over the state. Plenty of children's activities and good food make it a family-friendly occasion.

Leaving Naples, take a little side trip to visit **Sebago Lake State Park** by turning left off Route 302 West just after the swing bridge. Follow the signs to the park. There's everything you need here for a busy afternoon—hiking trails, picnic areas, and swimming in Sebago Lake, Maine's deepest

NAPLES

The town of Naples got its name because early residents thought the shape of the curving bay resembled that of the Italian city.

Sebago Lake from Migis Lodge in South Casco

and second-largest lake. If you didn't see the Songo Lock by boat, you can follow the signs and park nearby to take a look.

In nearby South Casco—reach it by heading east on Route 302 for 6.5 miles—you'll find **Migis Lodge,** among the last of the Maine resorts that once welcomed generations of the same families year after year for the summer season. Some families still continue this annual tradition, but every summer new visitors discover Migis, where you can be active from dawn to dusk (or from Chinese yoga on the front lawn to a sunset sail). The grounds slope down to Sebago Lake, and there's hardly a spot on the property that doesn't have a picturesque view. The atmosphere is completely laid back while still retaining some traditions from back in the day: A very civilized cocktail hour is followed by a leisurely dinner to which men are asked to wear jackets—a requirement that's cheerfully adhered to, often with a jacket tossed over Bermuda shorts. For some reason, young boys who wouldn't be caught dead in a jacket at home seem excited to don one and join the grownups for dinner; however, the lodge wisely offers other dining options for fidgety toddlers and their families.

When you're ready, return to Route 302 and turn north onto Route 35 just east of Naples and enjoy a scenic ride beside Long Lake to the pretty village of **Harrison** in the foothills of the White Mountains. Such a tiny place may seem an incongruous spot for a summer theater, but **Deertrees Theatre** has a well-deserved reputation as "a jewel in the Maine woods." Built in 1936 by famed opera coach Enrica Clay Dillon, the Adirondack-style wooden building, now listed on the National Register of Historic Places, has near-perfect acoustics and an impressive stage. In its early days, such luminaries as Talullah Bankhead, Ethel Barrymore, and Rudy Vallee graced the stage; today's performances include everything from Broadway plays to "wicked good" evenings of Yankee humor. The season is short—just eight weeks—but catch a performance if you can. You might make it an evening out by also having dinner at the **Olde Mill Tavern,** a gem of a place in its own right.

To continue on to **Norway,** turn right on Route 117. Little Norway was once known around the world for the quality of its snowshoes. A local maker provided snowshoes for Admiral Peary's 1909 North Pole expedition, and a Norway factory supplied most of the snowshoes used by the military in World War II. Today the town is best known for its gingerbread-trimmed homes and other attractive architecture. Some buildings date back to the 1800s, but most are more recent, having been constructed following a massive fire in 1894. Walking-tour booklets are available in downtown stores. A tour highlight is the handsome **Norway Library,** designed in the 1930s in neoclassic style by well-known Boston architect William B. Coffin.

A STOP TO SMELL THE FLOWERS

A side trip to South Paris will bring you to the **McLaughlin Garden,** blazing in a riot of color from May through September. If you're a gardener, you'll be impressed by what talented people with very green thumbs can coax forth from the rocky soil of Maine. A little café on the premises gives visitors a chance to sit among the blooms and simply enjoy the moment. Acknowledging that all gardeners need a sense of humor, the chef serves a special Blue Day soup only on days when rain threatens. You can get here from downtown Norway by continuing 1 mile east on Route 117.

If you're in town for breakfast or lunch, **Café Nomad** on Main Street serves up blueberry pancakes and hearty sandwiches, and if you should find yourself in Norway on the second weekend in July, you'll want to attend the annual **Norway Arts Festival**. Small-town New England at its best and friendliest, here you'll be treated to lectures, dance and music performances, poetry readings, art shows, puppet-making workshops, and plenty of down-home food such as lobster rolls and chicken potpie.

SCRIBNER'S MILLS

A brief detour just before the village of Harrison will bring you to **Scribner's Mills,** a reconstructed 1847 water-powered sawmill where volunteers still make wooden items using original equipment. If you've ever wondered how house shingles are shaped or how wooden barrels get their curved sides and perfect, tight-fitting covers, you can learn all about it here. During the first weekend in

Heavy-duty machinery is still in use at Scribner's Mill in Harrison.

August, a Back to the Past celebration includes antique car and truck demonstrations, candle-dipping workshops, horseshoeing and ox-pulling demonstrations, musical performances, and a pig roast. The mill cranks up all its machinery, and it's quite enlightening to see all that could once be accomplished with the two basic ingredients of water power and determination.

Leaving Norway on Route 118 West, turn left on Route 37 to continue to Waterford, with its attractive town green and Colonial homes on the banks of Keoka Lake. You'll spot public beaches where you can stop for a swim. If you're planning a weekend in the area, this might be a convenient time to take a break in your trip, which will soon bring you into busier Fryeburg and Bridgton. Try the beautiful **Lake House Bed & Breakfast and Restaurant,** built in the 1790s, where you can listen to the haunting call of loons on the lake outside your bedroom window.

Leaving Waterford on Route 35 North, you'll meander through some other small towns. Stop at the intersection of Routes 5 and 35 to see one of Maine's most-photographed landmarks, a road sign pointing the way to China, Sweden, Mexico, and other seemingly international destinations—all of which, like Norway, lie within Maine's borders. Turn left on Route 5 and travel on through **Stoneham**, **North Lovell**, and **Center Lovell**, where antiques shops abound. Try **William Doyle Antiques** in Center Lovell for furniture, cast-iron objects, china, and paintings.

> ### WHAT'S IN A NAME?
> Still part of Massachusetts in 1795, when they petitioned for incorporation, citizens of Norway intended to name their town *Norage*, an Abenaki word meaning "falls." Through some kind of miscommunication, authorities in Boston heard, or read, "Norway" instead, and Norway it became.

The big draw for many visitors to bucolic Lovell—population just under one thousand—is funky little **Ebenezer's Pub,** where you can quaff some of the world's finest beers—including Black Albert, made just for the pub—in an unlikely venue tucked away in the middle of the Maine woods. The pub can be a little difficult to find. It's just off Route 5 on Allen Road (near the golf course). Watch closely for signs. Beer lovers come from all over the country to choose among several hundred varieties of Belgian beers along with standard American brews. That huge assortment of Belgian beers and ales, including 35 on tap, has brought accolades to Ebenezer's from beer magazines naming it the best beer pub in the world. You can eat lunch or dinner, too, and perhaps watch a soccer game on the pub's TV or just chat with other beer lovers, some of whom make regular pilgrimages here.

Thus refreshed, continue on to **Fryeburg** from Lovell by proceeding south on Route 5. For proof that the family farm is alive and well in Maine, stop at the **Weston Farm** on Route 113 North, where six generations of

Westons have farmed the land. The farmstand where you can buy Maine crafts, jams, jellies, maple syrup, or a pie to finish off a picnic lunch was part of the original 1799 homestead.

The Saco River flows by the farm, and if that gives you the urge to get out on the water, this may be the time to try canoeing or kayaking. **Saco River Canoe** in Fryeburg can supply everything you need. The Saco is usually a gentle waterway, and as you paddle along you'll spot plenty of birds, including herons, as well as turtles and other small wildlife. You can overnight at the **Admiral Peary House** on Elm Street, where the discoverer of the North Pole once laid his head.

For more than 160 years the **Fryeburg Fair** has been a highlight of the harvest season, always held the first week in October. You can watch the judging of everything from fruits, vegetables, and knitting, to pigs, dairy cows, and draft horses, stuff yourself with cotton candy, deep-fried turkey legs, and corn dogs (preferably not just before you whirl around on the midway rides), and enjoy entertainment that includes bluegrass groups and barbershop quartets. There's a woodsmen's day, with old-time manly feats of strength like ax throwing and log rolling, and there's even a hurdy-gurdy player accompanied by a live monkey. The more than 330,000 people who attend each year can't be wrong: if it's been a while since you've enjoyed a real old-fashioned country fair with all the trimmings, the Fryeburg Fair is the real deal.

From Fryeburg, turn left onto Route 302 to **Bridgton**. The many lakes and ponds in Bridgton have made it a popular place for summer camps, so expect to see campers and lanyard-bedecked counselors out hiking or sightseeing. If you should come here in winter, there is pleasant, if not terribly challenging, skiing at **Shawnee Peak**. On your left, just before you enter Bridgton from Fryeburg, you'll come to the tiny **Rufus Porter Museum** dedicated to the versatile inventor, musician, poet, painter of landscape murals, and founder of *Scientific American,* who lived for a while in the area and briefly attended Fryeburg Academy. Throughout his long life (1792–1884) Porter was curious, restless, and creative, holding at least one hundred patents, including one for a revolving rifle that he ultimately sold to Samuel Colt. In New England, however, Porter is best

HOW HOT WAS IT?

On July 10, 1911, the temperature in North Bridgton reached 105 degrees, the hottest temperature ever recorded in Maine's history.

The Rufus Porter Museum in Bridgton

known for the extraordinary landscape wall murals he painted on the walls of private homes between 1825 and 1845, a number of which are on display in the museum. Occasionally an old home being remodeled reveals a landscape beneath layers of wallpaper, relatively easy to identify as the work of Porter because of the artist's departure from the classic themes then in vogue. Inspired by the natural world around him, he painted with bright colors and distinctive brushwork and his work is much admired and sought after today. The museum is a little gem that many travelers shoot past without realizing what they're missing.

The Lakes Region has long attracted artists and craftspeople, more than 60 of whom display their work at **Gallery 302** on Main Street, a cooperative fine-art gallery where you will find jewelry, paintings, ceramics, glass, woven baskets, and lots more. Everything in the gallery was created by artists from western Maine and eastern New Hampshire.

There's no lack of nostalgia in this part of Maine, and if you're a fan of old-fashioned diners, you won't want to miss **Ricky's Diner** on Main Street, where you can order pancakes and hash browns for dinner if you're so inclined. If you're of a certain age, you may remember drive-in movies, either heading off to them in your pj's with your parents or cramming as many teenage friends as possible into your car for an evening that usually involved very little film watching. At the height of their popularity in the late 1950s, there were more than four thousand drive-in theaters in the country. Today, fewer than four hundred remain, four of them in Maine. One of those is here in Bridgton. **The Bridgton Twin-Screen Drive-In** on Route 302 east of the village opened on Memorial Day 1957 and has been popular ever since with tourists and locals alike. If you're staying overnight in the area, just grab a bucket of popcorn and a few candy bars and settle in to find yourself transported back to a more carefree and simple time.

If it's time to return to the bright lights of Portland, just continue east on Route 302 for about an hour.

IN THE AREA

Dining

Café Nomad, 450 Main Street (Route 117), Norway. Phone: 207-739-2249; www.cafenomad.com. Breakfast foods, a variety of teas and coffees, cold beverages like sarsparilla and blueberry soda, and hearty wraps and sandwiches. Closed Sun. Inexpensive.

Ebenezer's Pub, 44 Allen Road, Lovell. Phone: 207-925-3200; www.ebenezerspub.net. Locals, businesspeople, and tourists convene in this laid-back, family-friendly pub where you can also have a tasty lunch or dinner—everything from sandwiches and chili to steak and chicken. Prices for food and beer are generally moderate, but some beers are expensive (the house specialty, the Belgian-made Black Albert, runs around $14 a bottle), so check prices before you order.

Lake House B&B and Restaurant, 686 Waterford Road, Waterford. Phone: 207-583-4182; www.lakehousemaine.com. Excellent food in a tranquil lakeside setting. Dinner only. Seasonal hours; call or check website for details. Moderate.

Olde Mill Tavern, 56 Main Street, Harrison. Phone: 207-583-9077; www.oldemilltavern.com. Excellent food and drink in the main restaurant or informal tavern. Dinner only. Moderate.

Ricky's Diner, 257 Main Street, Bridgton. Phone: 207-647-2499. Diner specials with an emphasis on seafood. Inexpensive.

Accommodations

Admiral Peary House, 27 Elm Street, Fryeburg. Phone: 207-935-3365; www.admiralpearyhouse.com. The former home of Arctic explorer Admiral Peary is now a tranquil bed & breakfast. Moderate; includes a full breakfast.

Augustus Bove House (bed & breakfast), 11 Sebago Road (corner of Routes 302 and 114), Naples. Phone: 1-888-806-6249; www.naplesmaine .com. Historic inn built in 1850; all modern amenities. Moderate; includes breakfast.

Chandler House B&B, 337 Intervale Road (Route 231), New Gloucester. Phone: 207-926-5502; www.chandlerhouse-bedandbreakfast.com. A peaceful setting and a choice of rooms or guest cottages. Inexpensive; includes a hearty breakfast.

Lake House B&B and Restaurant, 686 Waterford Road, Waterford. Phone: 207-583-4182; www.lakehousemaine.com. Moderate; includes full breakfast.

Migis Lodge, at Sebago Lake, off Route 302 (follow signs), South Casco. Phone: 207-655-4524; www.migis.com. A full-service resort offering a range of activities including swimming, sailing, kayaking, canoeing, waterskiing, hiking, tennis, yoga, and a variety of activities for children. Fitness center on the premises. Rustic, well-appointed cabins with all amenities. Expensive; rates include most activities and three meals daily. Reservations are a must.

Attractions and Recreation

Bridgton Twin-Screen Drive-In, Route 302, Bridgton. Phone: 207-647-8666. Admission (per person): Ages 12 and up, $7.50; 5–11, $5; under 5, free. Minimum charge of $15 per vehicle on Fri., Sat., and on Sun. holidays.

Deertrees Theatre, 156 Deertrees Road, Harrison. Phone: 207-583-6747; www.deertreestheatre.org. Season runs from late June through early

Sept. A small refreshment stand sells drinks and snacks; you're also welcome to picnic on the grounds. Check website for performances and ticket prices.

Fryeburg Fair, Route 5 (0.75 mile north from the intersection with Route 302), Fryeburg. Phone: 207-935-3268; www.fryeburgfair.com. Check website or call for exact dates. Admission: Adults, $10; children under 12, free; seniors free on Tues.

Maine Wildlife Park, Route 26, Gray. Phone: 207-657-4977, Ext. 1; www.state.me.us/ifw/education/wildlifepark. Open daily 9:30–4:30 (last admission); visitors may stay until 6. Park is open mid-May through Veterans Day. Admission: Ages 13–60, $7; children 4–12 and seniors, $5; under 3, free. A small store sells snacks, beverages, and souvenirs.

Norway Arts Festival, on (and near) Main Street, Norway. Opens the Thursday before the second weekend in July and runs through the weekend. Information and schedule: www.norwayartsfestival.com.

Norway Library, 248 Main Street, Norway. Phone: 207-743-5309; www.norway.lib.me.us. Ongoing events including art exhibitions and readings to which the public is welcome. Open every day except Sun.

Rufus Porter Museum, 67 North High Street (Route 302), Bridgton. Phone: 207-647-2828; www.rufusportermuseum.org. Displays of mural paintings by Rufus Porter and works by other artists, as well as lectures and classes. Coordinated by volunteers, so if making a special trip here, it's best to call ahead to be sure the museum is open. Usual hours are Wed.–Sat. from 12–4, from late June through early Sept., then Thurs.–Sat., 12–4, until early Oct. Call or check website for exact dates. Admission: Adults, $8; seniors, $7; ages 15 and under, free.

Sabbathday Shaker Village, 707 Shaker Road, New Gloucester. Phone: 207-926-4597; www.shaker.lib.me.us. Visitors welcome Memorial Day through Columbus Day, Mon.–Sat., 10–4:30, and at Sunday services. Six of the community's 18 buildings can be visited on guided tours. Admission: Adults, $6.50; children 6–12, $2; under 6, free.

Scribner's Mills, 244 Scribner's Mill Road, Harrison. Phone: 207-583-6455; www.scribnersmill.org. Open Sat. 1–4 from Memorial Day weekend through Labor Day weekend and during the first weekend in August for the Back to the Past celebration. Free admission; donations welcome and go toward continuing restoration of the mill.

Sebago Lake State Park, 11 Park Access Road, Casco. Phone: 207-693-6613; www.maine.gov/cgi-bin/online/doc/parksearch/details.pl?park_id =26. Open May 1 to mid-Oct. Boating, swimming at a 0.5-mile-long sandy beach, and fishing in Maine's deepest and second largest lake. Excellent hiking. Admission (day pass): Adults, $6.50; seniors, $2.

Shawnee Peak, 119 Mountain Road, Bridgton. Phone: 207-647-8444; www.shawneepeak.com. Opens when the snow flies for winter skiing; rentals available. Check website for details.

Songo River Queen II, The Causeway (Route 302), Naples. Phone: 207-693-6861; www.songoriverqueen.net. Open daily from Mother's Day to Halloween. Food and beverages available on board. Daily trips of varying lengths range from $12–$25 for adults; from $6–$13 for children. Call or check website for special themed trips.

Shopping

Gallery 302, 112 Main Street, Bridgton. Phone: 207-647-2787; www .gallery302.org. Wonderful Maine seascapes and landscapes. Open daily.

William Doyle Antiques, Main Street (Route 5), Center Lovell. Phone: 207-925-1279. Fine quality antiques. Open in summer only, daily except Wed., 10–5; Sun. 12–5.

Weston Farm, Route 113 North, Fryeburg. Phone: 207-935-2567; www .westonsfarm.com. Open daily mid-May through Dec. 24.

Other Contacts

Causeway Marina, 780 Roosevelt Trail (Route 302), Naples. Phone: 207-693-6832; www.causewaymarina.com. Open daily 8:30–4:30. Power boats rented by the half or full day, or weekly. Call or visit the website for boat options and prices.

Saco River Canoe & Kayak, 1009 Main Street, Fryeburg. Phone: 207-935-2369; www.sacorivercanoe.com. Rates vary; call or see website for details.

The Thompson Ice House in South Bristol

CHAPTER

15

Maine: Damariscotta and the Pemaquid Peninsula

Estimated length: About 50 miles from Portland to Damariscotta. Plan on approximately 50 miles to tour the area.

Estimated time: About one hour from Portland to Damariscotta. You can drive through the area easily in a day, but plan a couple of days if you are interested in touring historic sites, getting in some beach time, or taking a ferry ride.

Getting there: From Portland, take I-295 North to Brunswick. Then take Route 1 North to the Damariscotta exit (Business Route 1).

Highlights: This is the Maine of a thousand posters and colorful postcards. The Maine of rockbound coasts, lobster boats, bald eagles soaring overhead, tiny island communities, and **Pemaquid Light**, which may be the most beautiful lighthouse of your travels. Explore the **Whaleback Midden** shell heaps left by Native Americans who lived here long before the first white settlers came calling, pop into art galleries, watch fishermen pass through a scenic swing bridge, or park the car for a day and enjoy a ferry ride to the artists' island of **Monhegan**. You may find yourself agreeing that life in Maine is, indeed, "The way life should be."

Let everyone else continue their frantic drive up Route 1 toward the high-profile communities of Camden and Bar Harbor. Wave goodbye and ease onto Business Route 1, catching a glimpse of evergreens and tall church spires in the distance. As you cross over the bridge that joins the small twin villages of **Newcastle** and **Damariscotta**, you'll feel life beginning to slow down to a manageable pace.

Long ago, this was the home of Abenaki Native Americans; Damariscotta, which hugs the banks of the tidal Damariscotta River, takes its name from "Madamescontee," their term for "the place with an abundance of alewives" (a type of herring). Seeing the quiet and charming village of Damariscotta today, it's difficult to envision a time when Native Americans and settlers fought to control the area, but history tells of major fighting during King Philip's War and the French and Indian War. Later, Damariscotta became a shipbuilding center; many of the large old homes along the water were built with profits from maritime pursuits.

Take some time to wander the picturesque downtown (there are public parking lots in back of the stores on both sides of Main Street). You'll enjoy wonderful little shops like **Serendipity House,** where you can pick up gifts for those not lucky enough to be traveling with you, and not one but two branches of **Reny's,** a popular Maine discount store where you can stock up on anything you might need for your trip, from clothing to reading glasses or a can of peanuts. Independent **Maine Coast Books & Café** is a great place to choose books to read at the beach or your evening lodging. Inside the bookshop, a little café sells coffee, pastries, and snacks. Grab a window table if you're a people watcher, because a big part of Damariscotta's attraction is its 1950s-meets-21st-century vibe. Old buildings with vintage signs blend almost seamlessly with newer construction. People stroll along the sidewalks, the post office is a popular meeting spot, and in summer there's always something going on—perhaps fresh flowers being sold from a brightly colored cart, a street festival, or local actors hurrying to rehearse a play at the historic **Lincoln Theater.** One of the town's most popular festivals is its annual **Damariscotta Pumpkinfest**, which kicks off several days before Columbus Day weekend and culminates in a pumpkin regatta during which the town's most flexible citizens climb into giant, hollowed-out pumpkin boats and try to outpaddle each other to cross a finish line. That race is for purists. There's another race for motorized pumpkins (really!) and their captains.

Among the old buildings in the downtown area is the **Chapman-Hall House**, Damariscotta's oldest surviving home, perched at the top of the hill on Main Street. Built by housewright Nathaniel Chapman around 1754, the post-and-beam center-chimney Cape once stood on 600 acres overlooking the town. Take a look at the keeping room, with its hearth and bake oven, and the traditional borning room. Original floorboards and beams run through much of the house. A later parlor with a fancy mantel shows how the house evolved over time as its owners' tastes and family needs changed. If you're interested in architecture, be sure to climb to the second floor, where you can get a good look at the post-and-beam construction and the roofing system. You'll emerge with a better understanding of the everyday life of the early residents of Damariscotta, and grateful for the 20th-century citizens who stepped up in 1960 to save the home from being razed to make room for a gas station.

If you'd like to have lunch or dinner nearby before continuing your journey, several excellent restaurants are within walking distance. The **Newcastle Publick House** in Newcastle, and **King Eider's Pub & Restaurant, Salt Bay Café,** and **Damariscotta River Grill** in Damariscotta are all good choices.

When you're ready, turn onto Route 129 opposite the Chapman-Hall House to begin your drive along the **Pemaquid Peninsula**. The word *Pemaquid* is thought to mean "a point of land" in the Abenaki language, and as you travel the convoluted road along this peninsula, which juts about 14.5 miles into the sea, you'll understand why.

After traveling about 3 miles from Damariscotta, you'll come to a fork in the road where the peninsula splits into two parts. Bear right on Route 129. After about 0.5 mile, you'll see signs for the **Walpole Meetinghouse** on Meetinghouse Road on your left, definitely worth a stop if you have an

---

ART BENEATH YOUR FEET

The art of rug hooking, which produced the colorful floor coverings so prevalent in old homes throughout New England, is thought to have originated in Maine and in northern New Hampshire, no doubt building on a skill already well known in England and in Europe. In early 19th-century New England, hooking was seen as a thrifty way to use up scraps of cloth. Rags were torn into strips and then pulled through a backing—usually burlap in country homes—to form a decorative design. During the bleak New England winters, rural women sometimes gathered together to hook rugs, much as they came together to quilt. Rug hooking was an affordable pastime, used up the household rags, provided a creative outlet, and resulted in something both utilitarian and decorative.

---

interest in colonial architecture. Built in 1772, the meetinghouse is all original, including its hand-sawed shingles and handmade nails. If it's open at the time of your visit, be sure to have a look at the gorgeous pulpit, built by ship's carpenters, and visit the paneled balcony where servants worshiped.

Back on Route 129, continue on toward the little fishing village of **South Bristol**, one of the last pristine fishing villages in midcoast Maine. Just before you enter the village, you'll see **Thompson Ice House** on your left. Two popular events take place here each year that help keep an old local tradition alive. In midwinter, ice is cut on the icehouse pond using the same old-fashioned tools that were used when citizens regularly cut ice and shipped it as far away as India and China. The development of refrigeration ended that era, but for many years the icehouse continued to serve South Bristol and nearby communities by providing ice for the fishing industry and for summer cottages without electricity. Hoisted seven tiers high into the icehouse by a pulley system, the huge ice blocks stay frozen throughout the summer. Even today locals sometimes purchase ice here for their personal use. Mostly, though, the winter ice-cutting event is a nod to the town's past. While the ice is being cut and stored, children skate on the far side of the pond, volunteers sell hot drinks and snacks, and townspeople gather for a break in the long Maine winter. Come summer, visitors join locals for the annual ice cream social on the icehouse grounds, enjoying home-baked goodies, music, and ice cream churned with ice from the winter's harvest. If you're not in town during one of these events, you're still welcome to park at the icehouse and take a look around.

Continuing along Route 129, just after the icehouse, you'll pass the **S Road School** on the right. Built in 1860, the one-room schoolhouse has recently been restored to its approximate appearance in the 1930s based on input from several South Bristol residents who went to school there.

If you'd like to sample the local seafood, upon entering the village turn left onto Thompson Inn Road and follow the signs to the **South Bristol Fisherman's Co-op.** Here you can indulge your love of steamed clams and lobsters as they should be eaten—outside on a picnic bench with gulls squawking overhead and lobstermen pulling up at the wharf to unload their catch.

The pride and joy of many South Bristol residents is the lovely old **swing bridge,** one of a few remaining in Maine, which opens as many as one hundred times a day during the summer months to let boats pass

South Bristol Harbor

through. The bridge spans the South Bristol Gut, separating mainland South Bristol from its island section. You may want to pull off for picture taking. The harbor is scenic to say the least, with working lobster boats passing by, fishing boats setting out to sea, and pleasure craft of all kinds bobbing at their moorings.

On the other side of the bridge lies **Rutherford Island**, home to about 120 year-round residents. Shortly after rumbling across the swing bridge you'll pass the **South Bristol Historical Society** on your left, where you can stop in for additional information about the history of the area. Farther up on your right you'll see a quintessential little white New England church. **Union Congregational Church**, more than one hundred years old, holds frequent public suppers, fairs, and other events, announcements of which are posted on signs around town.

Continue on Route 129 and turn right onto Coveside Road to **Christmas Cove**. Supposedly, the English explorer John Smith named Christmas Cove when he sailed into the harbor on Christmas Day, 1614. (Some his-

A beachcomber examines a find at low tide at Christmas Cove.

torians say there is no historical record to back this up, but hey, it's a good story and a great name.) In-season, sailboats and motor yachts are often tied up outside **Coveside Restaurant**, where you can enjoy drinks or a meal in the convivial bar and restaurant or sit on the rustic deck and watch ospreys and eagles soar overhead and all the activity in the marina. Sit back with a Maine microbrew in your hand and you may never want to leave.

In fact, if you've decided at this point that you don't want to leave yet, turn right upon exiting Coveside and head for the **Unique Yankee Bed & Breakfast.** It's a pleasant place to stay, and the owners tend a lovely rose garden that you're welcome to stroll through. Alternatively, turn left to West Side Road when you leave Coveside and watch for Sunset Loop Road on your left. Here, in summer, you'll find another good choice, the little **Sunset B&B,** with friendly owners, an inviting porch, and views of the Damariscotta River.

Near the corner of West Side Road and Route 129, **Island Grocery** on your right is a good stop for gourmet sandwiches and snacks, which you can take with you or enjoy at the picnic tables outside. Then turn left onto Route 129 and head back across the bridge. At the top of the hill, **Harborside Café** is a little sit-down restaurant and grocery store where you can enjoy a leisurely meal. The only eatery in town that's open all year, Harborside Café features down-home cooking like chowder and chicken potpie, all of it just-like-Mom-made delicious. Linger over coffee and the newspaper and mingle with the locals who come and go all day. If you need directions, ideas for things to do in town, or just want to chat with people with cool coastal Maine accents, this is the place.

Follow Route 129 about 5 miles to Harrington Road and turn right. After about 1.5 miles, on your left, you'll pass the **Harrington Meetinghouse**. Built in 1775 and nicely restored, the meetinghouse now contains a small museum with historic artifacts and photos. Like the Walpole Meetinghouse, it was built to serve the spiritual needs of settlers at nearby **Colonial Pemaquid**. Various events are held in the meetinghouse from time to time during the summer months.

At the end of Harrington Road, turn right onto Route 130. After about 2 miles, turn right onto Huddle Road, then after another 1.2 miles turn right onto Old Fort Road to the **Colonial Pemaquid State Historic Site**. Colonial Pemaquid has a long and interesting history as both a military and farming community. When only Native Americans roamed here, the village that is now Pemaquid was probably a seasonal fishing site. In 1614 Captain John Smith explored and mapped much of the area, and at some point between 1625 and 1629 English settlers arrived to establish a permanent, year-round colony that quickly became an important fur-trading center. The years that followed had their share of drama. A disgruntled English sea captain turned pirate named Dixie Bull raided the settlement in 1632, probably choosing it to plunder because it had become well known for its lucrative fur trade. Arriving unexpectedly in the harbor with a crew of toughs he had picked up in Boston, he pillaged and ultimately destroyed the settlement. The Pemaquid settlers regrouped, rebuilt, and carried on. Three years later, the ship *Angel Gabriel,* carrying settlers to the New World, sank nearby in a heavy storm. Those who survived lost all their belongings and were stranded for a while at Pemaquid, where they were aided by the settlers at what was by then a well-established farming community. Meanwhile, relationships with the local Native Americans with whom the settlers continued to trade began a slow descent from friendly to guarded to hostile. In 1676 Native Americans destroyed the settlement during King Philip's War.

Four years later, Fort Charles was completed to protect the reestablished English settlement from both the French and the Native Americans allied with them. The fort looked strong, with its seven cannons and wooden picket walls, but too few soldiers were on hand to protect it and it fell, completely destroyed, to Native Americans in 1689, at which point the British abandoned Pemaquid for three years.

In 1692 the British tried again, constructing Fort William Henry on the same site. Despite walls as high as 22 feet, 20 cannons, and a force of 60 soldiers, the fort fell a few years later as Native Americans retaliated for cruel treatment by the English, who once again abandoned the site.

Thirty-three years passed before the English built a third and final fort at Pemaquid, constructing Fort Frederick in 1729 and abandoning it in 1759. Townspeople destroyed it in 1775 to prevent British troops from occupying it during the American Revolution. Several years later, a home, now known as the Fort House, was built close to the ruins of Fort Frederick, and a 300-acre farm was established on the grounds.

The Fort William Henry you can visit today is a partial reconstruction of the second fort, using some materials from Fort Frederick. It contains a number of interpretive panels that give the history of the settlement. You can also visit the Fort House, whose parlor room is decorated in early 19th-century style. Be sure to walk around the grounds, where there are fourteen stone cellar holes from various times in the village's history and an old cemetery with stones dating back to the early 1700s. The on-site museum and visitors center has information on special events, which often include costumed interpreters, lantern walks, and lectures by archaeologists, who continue to carry out excavations here.

Leave Colonial Pemaquid on Old Fort Road, then continue on to Snowball Hill Road for about 300 yards to reach **Pemaquid Beach Park,** where you can go for a walk or a swim or bask in the sun on the crescent-shaped beach. While you're in this area, you won't want to miss **Pemaquid Lighthouse,** so when you leave the beach, take Snowball Hill Road to **New Harbor,** turn right on Route 130, and drive to the end, where you'll enter **Pemaquid Lighthouse State Park.**

Along with a three-masted schooner from Maine's windjammer fleet, the iconic Pemaquid Lighthouse was chosen to represent Maine on the

Fort William Henry at the Colonial Pemaquid State Historic Site

state quarter. Built in 1835, the light in the 38-ft. stone lighthouse tower flashes every six seconds and can be seen 14 miles out at sea. The tower is open to the public (not recommended for small children because of the steep stairs) and offers a panoramic view of the Atlantic Ocean crashing on the rocks below. Part of the former keeper's house—home to the lighthouse keeper and his family in the days before lighthouses were automated—is now a charming Fisherman's Museum where you can learn more about the maritime history of the area. Also on the grounds are an oil house and a small tower that housed the fog bell used as an adjunct to the lighthouse's flashing beacon in especially treacherous weather. Across from the tower, the **Pemaquid Group of Artists** has built an art gallery showcasing the work of many local artists during the summer months.

The Lighthouse Park setting is so majestic that artists and photographers flock to the bluff, and many weddings are held here. Sit for a while and enjoy the scenery or have a picnic—several picnic tables are scattered

Pemaquid Light

around—and if you are surefooted, take a walk on the rocks, keeping well away from the water. Even on the most seemingly calm days, rogue waves can roar in at any time, sweeping everything in their path out to sea. If you're traveling here in the warm-weather months, have a meal or ice cream at the little **Sea Gull Shop** right next to the park.

Leaving Lighthouse Park, take Route 130, where you will pass the elegant **Bradley Inn.** You can stay overnight here, or stop for a special-occasion dinner. Continue on and turn right onto Route 32 to the harbor, where you'll find one of the peninsula's most popular restaurants. The opening of **Shaw's** restaurant each year signals the start of summer for many locals and visitors. Downstairs you can watch lobsters being hauled in by the New Harbor fleet. Take a peek at the holding tanks, where on occasion you can spot an unusual multicolored lobster. Upstairs you can eat your fill of fresh lobsters, steamers, and fried clams in a classic Maine setting. If you choose to eat on the deck, don't turn your back on your food. The ever-ravenous seagulls pounce in seconds. The downstairs bar is a lively spot, especially on weekends. Film buffs with sharp eyes and good memories may recognize the wharf from the 1999 movie *Message in a Bottle,* starring Kevin Costner. Many of the waterfront scenes were filmed right here, and chances are, some of the locals eating at the tables beside you were extras.

The dock at Shaw's is also the departure point for the ***Hardy III,*** a ferry that will take you on a day trip to **Monhegan,** the artists' island. Work this ferry ride into your trip plans if you possibly can—you definitely won't regret it. Leave the car behind, but not in Shaw's parking lot. The ferry has its own parking lot about a five-minute walk from the wharf. If you just can't squeeze in a day trip to Monhegan, try to hop on the *Hardy III* for a lighthouse-viewing excursion or a seal-watching or puffin-watching trip. The entire hour-long ride out to Monhegan is one beautiful vista after another, and along the way you're likely to spot minke whales, harbor seals,

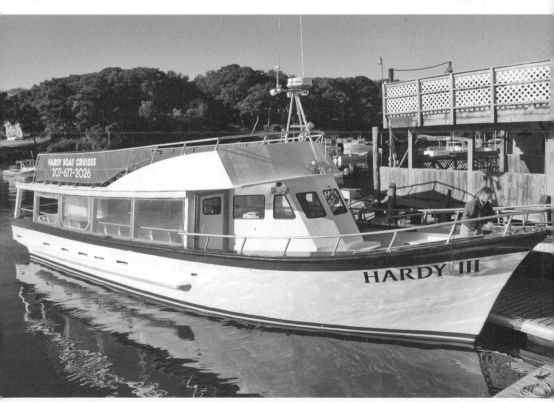

Capt. Al Crocetti prepares the Hardy III *for a trip to Monhegan Island.*

harbor porpoises, cormorants, and puffins in-season. Occasionally a humpback whale passes by. Owner and ferry captain Al Crocetti does a bang-up job of narrating the passing scenery and calling passengers' attention to area wildlife.

From the time the ferry arrives at the Monhegan dock, you'll know you're in a special place. Lying about 10 miles out to sea from New Harbor, Monhegan was once inhabited by Native Americans who used it as a base for summer fishing. It's thought that several European explorers passed by the island, including Giovanni da Verrazano and Samuel de Champlain, but it was Captain John Smith, exploring the coast in 1614, who brought it the most attention. Today Monhegan is home to a year-round community of about 65 people, with many island families actively engaged in lobstering in the winter months when many other lobster fishermen have put away their traps for the season. Only the small village (no paved roads, no streetlights, limited cell phone service) is developed; the rest of the island is thick woods and meadows, crisscrossed with about 12 miles of trails. Some are easy walking; others are rugged and lead to some of the highest and most dramatic cliffs on the Maine coast. If you plan to hike, be sure to pick up a trail map on the ferry or at one of the island stores, and remember that there are no doctors, hospitals, or pharmacies on the island. In an emergency, you can call 911—assuming your cell phone functions out here—but all but limited assistance has to come from the mainland. In short, this would not be a good place to test your physical limits.

On a day trip to Monhegan, you'll only be on the island for a few hours, but that's time enough to walk to the lighthouse and its museum, explore

---

WHAT DO I DO WITH THIS CLAM?

In Maine, you'll often find "steamers" on the menu, and always as part of a traditional lobster dinner. Although lobsters are usually accompanied by a bib or a placemat that explains how to eat them, first-time eaters of steamers are often stymied. Maine steamers are small, oval, soft-shelled clams. About a pound per person is usual as a starter, and they are typically served with a cup of broth and a cup of melted butter. Clams are sandy when dug out of the muddy clam flats, so they are purged for a day or two before steaming. The broth is only for dipping, just in case a few grains of sand remain. Remove the loose skin, or membrane, from the neck and, holding the clam by the neck, dip it first in broth, then in butter, and enjoy.

---

a bit of the forest at Cathedral Woods, and wander through the village with its picturesque church, tiny schoolhouse (yes, island children go to school here), and art galleries. You could swim at Swim Beach, but there are no changing facilities. Still, it's fun to roll up your pant legs and splash around a bit. For lunch there are several choices, including **The Barnacle** at the wharf. When you depart on the ferry, you may notice islanders jumping off the dock and into the water as the ferry pulls out, their way of saying goodbye and hoping you'll come back again someday.

When you're ready to travel on from New Harbor, continue on Route 32 North to the little village of **Round Pond**. Its harbor is one of the coast's most charming and a great place to watch lobstermen heading out to sea. In the early 1800s Round Pond was a farming and fishing community, and fishing has remained important down through the years. By the mid-19th-century three shipyards were in operation here, and by the turn of the century the village had been discovered as a tourist destination, with steamships transporting vacationers for stays that often lasted

AT THE EDGE OF THE SEA

Rachel Carson, biologist, environmentalist, and author of *The Edge of the Sea* and *Silent Spring*, conducted much of her research for *The Edge of the Sea* in a tidal pool located beside Route 32 between New Harbor and Round Pond. **The Rachel Carson Salt Pond Preserve** is now owned by The Nature Conservancy, which keeps the 0.25-acre tide pool open to the public. It's an especially nice place to stop with children, who will have fun observing the various rock formations as well as sea life in the shallow pools of salt water. Among the rocks are gray granulite, formed some 420 million years ago. In the pool, watch for a variety of seaweeds, periwinkles, barnacles, mussels, hermit crabs, and other little sea creatures.

most of the summer. If you happen to be here on the Fourth of July, don't miss the unique town parade, complete with special entries like politically themed floats and the "Tacky Tourists," a dance group of sorts that cavorts around with folding chairs. Afterward, there's a big chicken barbecue in the town center.

If it's been a long time since you've seen an old-fashioned country store, you'll find one in Round Pond at the **Granite Store**, selling penny candy (costing somewhat more than a penny), souvenirs, decorative items for the home, local crafts, and ice cream. **The Inn at Round Pond,** in a lovely 1830s building, is near the harbor and open all year for a real get-away-from-it-all experience. Mostly, you'll just have fun poking around the town and enjoying the scenery and the variety of architectural styles, including a number of mansard-roof homes.

Leave Round Pond on Route 32 North and after about 4 miles, turn left onto Biscay Road. Continue on to Damariscotta, and at the traffic light, turn right onto Business Route 1. When you see the sign for the **Whaleback Midden,** pull into the small parking lot.

Middens are, essentially, dumps, and when found intact they reveal a lot about the people who used them. The Whaleback Midden is thought to be some twenty-five hundred years old, a huge shell heap where the Abenaki tossed the remnants of countless oyster dinners. Although once more than 30 feet deep, in the late 19th century, a good portion of the Whaleback Midden was shoveled up so the oyster shells could be ground into chicken feed. One of several middens along the Damariscotta River, Whaleback got its name from its original humped shape. Unfortunately, there's no resemblance to a whale today. An easy trail leads to the midden, and along the way some explanatory panels give its history.

You may want to wind up your tour at nearby **Round Top Ice Cream**, long a local favorite, before returning to downtown Damariscotta and beginning your journey back to Portland.

THE HERMIT OF MANANA

Across the harbor from Monhegan, you'll see the tiny, uninhabited island of Manana (rhymes with banana), once the site of a Coast Guard fog station. From the 1920s until his death in 1975, it was also the home of Ray Phillips, "the Hermit of Manana." A well-educated New Yorker, Phillips, for reasons unknown, abruptly left his life in the city behind and moved to the barren rock, where he tended a few sheep, kept a gander as his constant companion, and lived in apparently blissful isolation in a shack he built of found odds and ends. He rowed across to Monhegan to buy the necessities of life, and when he grew old and ill, Monhegan residents saw to it that he had everything he needed.

Also on Manana are a few rune-like markings that some attribute to early Viking explorers. Most experts, however, think they are just natural scratches formed by the action of wind and sea. You can usually find someone on Monhegan who will take you out to Manana by skiff for a small fee. Ask him or her to stick around until you've had a quick look or agree on a time to be picked up. The ferry back to the mainland waits for no one.

IN THE AREA

Accommodations

Bradley Inn, Route 130, New Harbor. Phone: 1-800-942-5600; www .bradleyinn.com. An elegant inn and spa. Expensive; full breakfast and afternoon tea included.

Inn at Round Pond, 1442 Route 32, Round Pond. Phone: 207-809-7386; www.theinnatroundpond.com. Open year-round. Moderate.

Sunset B & B, 16 Sunset Loop, South Bristol. Phone: 207-644-8849; Open May–Oct. Kayakers can launch directly across from the B&B. Very inexpensive.

Unique Yankee Inn, 53 Coveside Road, South Bristol. Phone: 1-866- 644-1502; www.uniqueyankeeofmaine.com. Dinner available for guests only; lobster dinners in summer, other choices in the off-season. See web- site for details. Inexpensive.

Dining

Anchor Inn, Anchor Inn Road, Round Pond. Phone: 207-529-5584; www.redplatecatering.com. A local favorite open from Mother's Day through Columbus Day weekend. Fresh fish is a specialty. Moderate.

Bradley Inn, Route 130, New Harbor. Phone: 1-800-942-5600; www .bradleyinn.com. Open for dinner; seasonal hours, check website for details. Moderate to expensive.

Coveside, 105 Coveside Road, South Bristol. Phone: 207-644-8282; www .covesiderestaurant.com. Eat in the pub, the restaurant, or outside over- looking the water. Open late spring through early fall for lunch and din- ner. Moderate.

Damariscotta River Grill, 155 Main Street, Damariscotta. Phone; 207- 563-2992; www.damariscottarivergrill.com. Good food, terrific oysters, and a well-chosen wine list. Open for lunch, dinner, and brunch on Sun. Moderate.

Harborside Café, 2077 Route 129, South Bristol. Phone: 207-644-8751. Open daily for all three meals throughout the year. Inexpensive.

Island Grocery, 12 West Side Road, South Bristol. Phone: 207-644-8552; www.islandgrocery.net. A few inside seats and outdoor picnic tables. Upscale food including free-range roasted chickens, fresh breads, pastries, and homemade ice cream. Open daily Memorial Day weekend until early fall. Moderate to expensive.

King Eider's Pub & Restaurant, 2 Elm Street (corner of Main and Elm), Damariscotta. Phone: 207-563-6008; www.kingeiderspub.com. A casual pub downstairs; a quieter restaurant upstairs, both serving fresh Damariscotta oysters, spicy chicken wings, and very good crab cakes. Moderate.

Newcastle Publick House, 52 Main Street, Newcastle. Phone: 207-563-3434; www.newcastlepublickhouse.com. A cheerful bar fronts an excellent restaurant with a well-balanced menu. Oysters from the nearby Damariscotta River are a big draw. Open for lunch and dinner. Inexpensive to moderate.

Round Top Ice Cream, 526 Main Street, Damariscotta. Phone: 207-563-5307. Rich and delish. A must stop in-season. Open daily from late spring through fall.

Salt Bay Café, 88 Main Street, Damariscotta. Phone: 207-563-3302; www.saltbaycafe.com. Popular with locals. In addition to the regular menu there's a separate large menu of vegetarian and vegan choices. Open daily for all three meals. Inexpensive to moderate.

Sea Gull Shop, 3119 Bristol Road, New Harbor. Phone: 207-677-2374; www.seagullshop.com. A charming little restaurant reminiscent of Grandma's kitchen looks out over the Atlantic Ocean on one side and the Pemaquid Lighthouse on the other. Bring your own adult beverages. Down-home New England cooking at all three meals; adjoining gift shop, too. Seasonal hours from early spring through early fall; check website for open hours during the time you'll be there. Moderate.

Shaw's Fish and Lobster Wharf, 129 Route 32, New Harbor. Phone: 207-677-2200. Indoor and outdoor dining for lunch and dinner. Terrific views. Moderate.

South Bristol Fisherman's Co-op, 35 Thompson Inn Road, South Bristol. Phone: 207-644-8224. Lobsters, clams, soft drinks, and snacks to eat overlooking the busy Gut. Inexpensive.

The Barnacle, Monhegan Island. Affiliated with the Island Inn across the road. Phone: 207-596-0371; www.islandinnmonhegan.com. Open for breakfast and lunch and into the late afternoon; eat there or pick up sandwiches for a picnic. Moderate.

Attractions and Recreation

Chapman-Hall House, Main Street, Damariscotta. Phone: 207-882-6817 (Lincoln County Historical Association). The home is listed on the National Register of Historic Places.

Colonial Pemaquid State Historic Site, Old Fort Road, New Harbor. Phone: 207-677-2423 (Apr.–Oct.); 207-624-6075 (off-season); www .friendsofcolonialpemaquid.org. Small fee charged.

Damariscotta Pumpkinfest, Damariscotta (various downtown locations). Contact: www.damariscottapumpkinfest.com. The October festival includes the decorative carving of giant pumpkins, which are later displayed along Main Street, a parade, music, a fun run, special kids' activities, plus the regatta at the Damariscotta River where participants attempt to paddle or drive their pumpkin boats to victory.

Hardy III, Hardy Boat Cruises, 132 Route 32, New Harbor. Phone: 1-800-278-3346; www.hardyboat.com. In summer, Monhegan trips depart New Harbor at 9 and 2, and leave Monhegan at 10:15 and 3:15. Light breakfast items, coffee, snacks, and wine and beer sold on board. Adults, $32; children 3–11, $18. Parking $3 per day, payable in advance by cash or check (no credit cards accepted for parking) at the marked lot. Check website for spring and fall schedule (ferry does not run in winter), and for schedule and rates for shorter cruises. Reservations are recommended for all cruises, especially in July and Aug.

Harrington Meetinghouse, 278 Harrington Road, Pemaquid. Information: www.colonialmeetinghouses.com/mh_harrington.shtml. Open in July and Aug., Mon., Wed., and Fri. from 2–4:30.

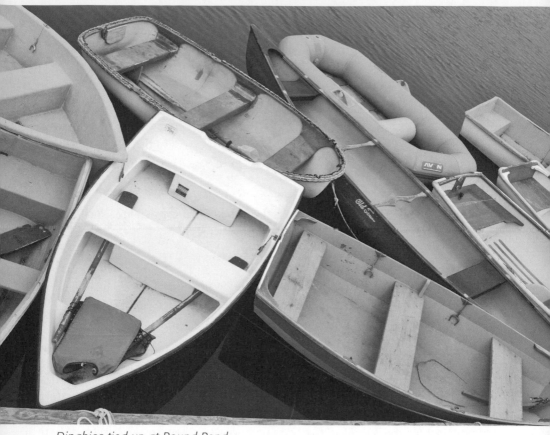

Dinghies tied up at Round Pond

Lincoln Theater, 2 Theatre Street, Damariscotta. Phone: 207-563-3424; www.lcct.org. Movies and plays throughout the year. Admission fees vary.

Pemaquid Beach Park, off Snowball Hill Road, New Harbor. Contact: www.bristolparks.org. Changing facilities, showers, snack bar, beach rentals, and a nature center with a touch tank in the pavilion. Seasonal fee, $4 per person; under 12, free. In the off-season, you can walk the beach at no charge.

Pemaquid Point Lighthouse Park and Pemaquid Point Lighthouse, New Harbor. Contact: www.bristolparks.org/lighthouse.htm. Park entrance, $2 per person during the warm-weather months; children under 12, free; no entrance fee in winter. Admission is free to lighthouse tower and museum; donations appreciated.

S Road School, Route 129 and S Road, South Bristol. Open July and Aug., Fri. from 1–4. No fee.

South Bristol Historical Society, 2124 Route 129, South Bristol. Phone: 207-644-1234; www.southbristolhistoricalsociety.org. Open Sun., 2–4, June–Sept.

Thompson Ice House, Route 129, South Bristol. Winter ice cutting held on Presidents' Day Weekend in Feb.; ice cream social held the Sun. closest to July 4. Open July and Aug. on Wed., Fri., and Sat., 1–4. Donations appreciated.

Union Congregational Church, Route 129 and Middle Road, South Bristol. Phone: 207-644-8242; www.tidewater.net/~ucsb.

Walpole Meeting House, Meetinghouse Road (off Route 129), South Bristol. Contact: www.colonialmeetinghouses.com/mh_walpole.shtml. Occasional events are held here; watch local newspapers for information.

Whaleback Midden, Business Route 1, Damariscotta, just north of the village. www.maine.gov/doc/parks/programs/history/whaleback. Wear sneakers or other sturdy footwear for the short, easy walk to the midden. Free admission.

Shopping

Maine Coast Book Shop & Café, 158 Main Street, Damariscotta. Phone: 207-563-3207; www.mainecoastbookshop.com. A wonderful combination of a well-planned bookstore and a friendly little café. Open daily.

Pemaquid Group of Artists Art Gallery, Pemaquid Lighthouse Park, New Harbor. Staffed by volunteers, the gallery is usually open from late May into the fall.

Reny's, 116 Main Street (clothing only) and 163 Main Street (everything else imaginable), Damariscotta. Phone: 207-563-5757 (clothing) or 207-563-3011; www.renys.com. Open daily.

Serendipity House, 93 Main Street, Damariscotta. Phone: 207-563-3331. Gift items, pottery, jewelry, children's toys and books, gourmet chocolates. Open daily.

Other Contacts

Monhegan Island information: www.monheganisland.com.

Saltwater Charters, Round Pond. Phone: 207-677-6229; www.saltwater-charters.com. Fish for fish or for lobsters or just relax and watch for seals aboard the 38-ft. *Paige Elizabeth.* The captain supplies fishing gear; bring your own food if you wish. Leaves from dock at Round Pond; call ahead for reservations and fees.

Other Resources

Connecticut Tourism. Phone: 1-888-Ctvisit; www.ctvisit.com.

Maine Office of Tourism. Phone: 1-888-624-6345; www.visitmaine.com.

Massachusetts Office of Tourism. Phone: 1-800-227-MASS; www.mass-vacation.com.

New Hampshire Office of Tourism. Phone: 603-271-2665; www.visit nh.gov.

Rhode Island Office of Tourism. Phone: 1-800-250-7384; www.visit rhodeisland.com.

Vermont Office of Tourism. Phone: 802-828-3237; www.vermont vacation.com.

About the Author

Born and raised near Boston, Karen Hammond is a twelfth-generation New Englander and intrepid traveler who has always been drawn to the unknown and unexpected—perhaps a legacy of her ancestors who traveled to the New World aboard the *Mayflower*. Her travel, food, and wine articles appear in major national and international publications and she is a popular conference speaker and lecturer. She currently lives in a fishing village on the coast of Maine.